TS

THE ST. LOUIS ART MUSEUM

HANDBOOK OF THE COLLECTIONS

PUBLISHED IN 1975 BY THE ST. LOUIS ART MUSEUM
FOREST PARK, ST. LOUIS, MISSOURI
ALL RIGHTS RESERVED

PRINTED AND BOUND IN GREAT BRITAIN BY
LUND HUMPHRIES, BRADFORD

TYPE SET IN TRUMP MEDIEVAL BY
ADRIAN TYPOGRAPHERS, ST. LOUIS

DESIGNED BY RICHARD S. CLEVELAND

THIS PROJECT IS SUPPORTED IN PART BY A GRANT
FROM THE NATIONAL ENDOWMENT FOR THE ARTS
IN WASHINGTON, D.C., A FEDERAL AGENCY.

LIBRARY OF CONGRESS CATALOGUE CARD NUMBER 75-18691

ISBN 0-89178-020-9

This edition of the handbook is the first to appear in more than twenty years. It includes over 850 illustrations of works of art added to the collection from about 1909 through 1974. Intended to present an overview of the Museum, the handbook includes many of its recognized masterpieces but it also reveals the broad diversity of the collections.

More than three-quarters of the works of art illustrated have been re-photographed. In every instance attributions were reconsidered by the curatorial staff in the light of recent scholarship and other data included in the illustration captions have been reviewed for accuracy. Dimensions are given in the metric system in accordance with current international practice. Because many excellent general and more specialized texts are now readily available to the Museum visitor it was decided to dispense with the brief art historical introductions which so often precede the various sections of a museum handbook.

In order to illustrate as many works of art as possible only brief captions could be used; this often required abbreviation of complete titles of purchase funds and modification of otherwise lengthy credit and media lines. Beginning on page 371 there is a formal listing of all purchase funds and of private or corporate donors who either gave the works of art illustrated or made available funds for their purchase. On the same page will be found the names of Museum Benefactors, most of whom also assisted the Museum in the development of its collections.

The preparation of this publication involved many members of the Museum staff and I would like to thank all those who were helpful. I am, however, particularly grateful to Mary-Edgar Patton, our registrar, to Wilfred T. Schone, the Museum's chief packer, and his assistants, William Kelly and Anthony Schlader, for their patience and care in handling works of art being moved for photography. Jack Savage, our photographer, and Louise Walker, our photography manager, devoted infinite patience and skill to obtaining photographs of the best quality. Without dedicated secretarial assistance the handbook would not exist and therefore I recognize the contributions made by Jo Ann Hayes and Susan Baerwald, curatorial secretaries, and by Evelyn Rullkoetter, my own secretary, who typed copy, checked spellings, and generally kept a sharp watch for the ever present possibility of error. Richard Gaugert, program coordinator, Christy B. Shreffler, public information officer, Reka Neilson Fisher, curatorial assistant, and Ann Abid, the Museum's librarian, also reviewed text, illustration captions, and otherwise made helpful suggestions. The work of checking information for works of art illustrated was performed by the curators; they also determined which works of art in their care were to be illustrated.

The final editing was the responsibility of Thomas L. Williams, the Museum's publications editor, and I am grateful for his meticulous attention to detail. Richard S. Cleveland, the Museum's associate curator for Oriental art and design coordinator, organized the content of the handbook and must be given full credit for its layout and design.

All of us on the Museum staff have reason to be indebted to the National Endowment for the Arts for it was through a grant made by this federal agency in 1974 that we were able to begin work on this project.

C.E.B.

CONTENTS

The purpose of this introductory essay is to set forth the history of The St. Louis Art Museum in terms of its collections and thereby, together with the illustrations, to remind the reader of what the Museum has been fortunate enough to have acquired over some sixty-five years. In the development of these collections, St. Louisans have played major roles by making bequests and gifts, and by providing funds for acquisitions. To refer to each of the donors individually is impossible in this brief text but many of their names will be found in relation to the illustrations.

The Museum's accessions records begin in 1909. In the first decade thereafter there seems to have been no particular plan for systematic purchasing, even though an apparent striving toward a cross-section of world art provided a general guideline for the disposition of such purchase funds as were available. After 1920 the collection began to increase in scope and quality so that today the Museum can lay claim to representing almost every major culture, often with works of art of genuine importance. However, at no time in its history has the Museum had substantial purchase funds at its command. In fact, as its annual reports spell out, these funds have been modest although in spite of this handicap the collections have grown impressively, through purchase, bequest, and by the receipt of gifts of prime importance.

At the end of 1974 The St. Louis Art Museum had in its collections 1,066 European and American paintings, 865 European and American watercolors and drawings, and 314 European and American sculptures, as well as numerous examples of European and American furniture, ceramics, glass and silver. It also had a surprisingly large and varied collection of textiles, exclusive of its outstanding collection of Near Eastern carpets. The Museum's print collection numbered some 4,000 impressions from the 15th century to the present. Representing civilizations beyond those of Europe and North America there is strength in the Far East, particularly in Chinese porcelains and bronzes, in Pre-Columbian and South Pacific cultures and in those of Central Africa.

The background for the Museum as it gradually emerged is well worth relating. On May 10, 1881, the first building devoted solely to art school and museum use was dedicated at the northwest corner of 19th and Locust Streets in an area then known as Lucas Place. The building was of limestone, with dark sandstone ornamentation, following a striking design developed by the prominent Boston architectural firm of Peabody and Stearns. The building was the gift of Wayman Crow, a St. Louis merchant and philanthropist, in memory of his only son Wayman Crow, Jr., who had died in England in 1878 at the age of twenty-two.

Because of Wayman Crow's interest in Washington University, for which he had been instrumental in obtaining a charter from the Missouri State Legislature during his term of office as a state senator, it was natural for him to visualize an art school and museum as a part of the university. To direct this newly founded enterprise known as the St. Louis School and Museum of Fine Arts, the services of Halsey Cooley Ives were engaged. Ives was soon joined by a number of well-known St. Louis artists to teach drawing and painting, among them Paul Harney, Howard Kretschmer, Holmes Smith, Edmund Engler and Carl Gutherz. In the museum part of the building a few original works of art were shown, including paintings by Charles Wimar, but the collections were mostly copies, such as casts of the Laocoon, Ghiberti's Baptistery doors and Peter Vischer's shrine of St. Sebald.

Halsey Cooley Ives was born in 1847, in the small town of Montour Falls, New York. In 1874, after spending several years in Nashville and then in the south and west where he gained experience as a designer and decorator, he came to St. Louis. Although a young man of recognized talent, Ives' true ability appears to have been in organizing and administering the art school and museum to serve the needs of Washington University. For Ives, always a dedicated teacher, the importance of art in everyday life was an article of faith and he devoted himself to promoting this conviction throughout the city. Ives later contributed his administrative skill to the World's Columbian Exposition in Chicago in 1893 and to the St. Louis World's Fair which, in 1903, was laid out on a lavish scale in Forest Park to commemorate the 100th anniversary of the Louisiana Purchase. The Fair was formally opened on April 30, 1904, when President Theodore Roosevelt pressed a gold telegraph key in the East Room of the White House, thus communicating with Fair officials gathered in the Park.

Halsey Ives devoted his energies to overseeing the plans for the art exhibitions at the Fair and most especially to the erecting on Art Hill, at the western end of the Park, of a fine arts pavilion designed by the well-known New York architect, Cass Gilbert. While his contribution to organizing the exhibitions was crucially important, as the Fair drew to a close Ives worked to bring about the transition from a temporary situation to one that would be permanent. Thus it was Ives who provided the foundation for future museum growth, independent of the art department of Washington University.

When the Fair closed in the fall of 1904 it was clear to all St. Louisans that its truly spectacular success had focused national and international attention on their city. Because of Ives' dedication and his organizational skills, the Fair had paid impressive tribute to the visual arts of many nations and paintings, sculpture and decorative art crowded the fine arts pavilion. Cass Gilbert's pavilion, in fact, consisted of four sections of which only the central one, constructed of Bedford gray limestone and Roman brick, was envisaged as a permanent structure. This section is the present Museum building. During the Fair it was flanked on the east and west by large temporary structures, with a free standing fourth structure on the south side intended for the display of sculpture.

Some two years after the Fair closed, the Cass Gilbert building was given by the Louisiana Purchase Exposition Company to the city for use as a municipal art museum, a move long anticipated by Ives and other St. Louisans. As the three temporary structures were demolished, work was begun to adapt the center section for museum purposes.

On March 7, 1907, the Missouri legislature took the unprecedented step of passing enabling legislation which gave St. Louis residents an opportunity to vote on a mill tax on real property for the support of an art museum. At that time no other state or city had made so dramatic a move to provide a broad base of support for a cultural institution. But even though St. Louisans by an overwhelming majority voted in favor of such a tax, appropriations for operations and purchases were not immediately forthcoming owing to certain legalities; nor was a board appointed in accordance with the law. This matter was dealt with over a period of time when interested parties acting on behalf of the Museum filed suit for the release by the city and its mayor of tax funds and for the appointment of the required nine man board. A decision favorable to the Museum was handed down by the Missouri Supreme Court during the October term of 1911. With its annual appropriation thus assured and a board appointed, the Museum was at last ready to begin the work that Ives had in mind.

By 1909 the Museum had been officially designated as the City Art Museum. As it was Ives who had worked so diligently to bring the new art museum into being he was rightfully appointed its first director. Its first president was a prominent St. Louisan, William K. Bixby, Chairman of the Board of the American Car and Foundry Company, and a collector of Far Eastern art who held the office until his death in 1931. The vice-president was David R. Francis, a merchant and former mayor of St. Louis, as well as a governor of Missouri and Secretary of the Interior under President Cleveland. As president of the St. Louis World's Fair, Francis had played a distinguished role. In 1916 President Wilson appointed him Ambassador to Russia, where he remained through two turbulent years.

Soon after 1909, under Bixby, Francis, and other members of the Board of Control, as the governing body was called, the task was begun of creating a permanent art museum for the benefit of St. Louis. Under successive presidents, of whom the last was Henry B. Pflager, this Board continued to define and oversee Museum policy until December 31, 1971. At that time, in accordance with the creation of the Metropolitan Zoological Park and Museum District voted into being on April 6, 1971, control of the Museum passed to a new Board, the Board of Commissioners, with George S. Rosborough, Jr., as its first president. This Board follows the pattern established by its predecessor. The new governing body is comprised of five City and five St. Louis County members. It is important to note that the Zoo/ Museum District was created through an act of legislation similar to that which in 1907 had technically established tax support for the Museum. In the 1971 vote both City and County residents were required to approve the measure. Having won approval, the Museum began operating under its new name, The St. Louis Art Museum, on January 1, 1972.

By 1909 Ives had accomplished his principal task, that of establishing a municipal tax-supported art museum housed in a building of handsome design occupying a prime location. To have unified so many conflicting points of view in creating the City Art Museum was no mean task and it remains as the most significant accomplishment in the life of the first director. Unfortunately, Ives did not live to see his Museum develop along the lines he had envisioned, as he died suddenly while on a visit to London in May,

1911. A bronze bust by the St. Louis sculptor Victor S. Holm is prominently displayed in the Museum, and through the kindness of Halsey Cooley Ives' granddaughter, his brilliantly executed portrait by Anders Zorn has been placed on long term loan.

Ives was well aware that the Museum could not remain static and that it was essential to plan early for future growth. Therefore, by 1908 there was already in existence an architectural plan proposing the extension of the Museum to the south, providing an auditorium, library, more exhibition space and other facilities. In 1916 Cass Gilbert drew up an even more elaborate scheme. Had this plan been carried out, it would have overshadowed Gilbert's original building while transforming the gently sloping contour of Art Hill into a series of formal terraces descending to a basin to connect visually the Museum with the Jefferson Memorial.

The further organization of the Museum and the development of its collections fell to Ives' successors, starting with his associate, Robert Allen Holland, who was appointed director in 1912. Not long after city funding of the Museum had begun the first purchases were made. Among those for 1913 was William Merritt Chase's *Still Life* (239). In 1915 two fine French 19th century pictures were bought, *Charing Cross Bridge*, by Claude Monet (162), and *The Reader*, by Edouard Manet (155). That same year saw the purchase of a number of pictures of quality by American artists such as Alexander Wyant, Julian Alden Weir and Willard Metcalf. In addition, a group of bronzes was acquired directly from Paul Manship, a young artist then at the beginning of a distinguished and productive career. Prints, too, were among the early acquisitions. These and other works of art provided the foundation for the Museum's now large American collection.

In 1916, with the purchase of several outstanding 17th century Dutch paintings, the Museum began to acquire works by European masters.

Among them was an exquisite portrait of *Jacob de Graeff* (101), given to Gerard Ter Borch, and Jan van Goyen's oil *Skating on the Ice Near Dordrecht* (98). The following year brought a number of interesting pictures from the collection of Mrs. Daniel K. Catlin, including works by artists who are once again beginning to find favor, such as Victor Gabriel Gilbert, Jean Charles Cazin, Alphonse Marie de Neuville and Jean Georges Vibert.

The W. K. Bixby Oriental Art Trust Fund was established in 1919. Because of the donor's personal interest in Far Eastern art and his travels to that part of the world, a wide range of Chinese and Japanese art, some of excellent quality, now began to appear in the exhibition galleries. Bixby's most distinguished purchase by far was made in Peking in 1919, when he acquired a scroll painting of *Fish Swimming Amid Falling Flowers* (289), which is believed to have been a part of the Imperial collections. This scroll, of Sung Dynasty origin, is recognized as being one of the finest paintings of its type in existence.

A major development in April, 1915, was the opening of the Richardson Memorial Library, occupying three galleries on the east side of the Museum. Halsey Cooley Ives had been eager to see a fine arts library established and it was Mary D. Richardson who, in honor of her husband, J. Clifford Richardson, bequeathed funds for its support. The cornerstone of the book collection was the purchase of some 4,000 volumes pertaining to art and architecture from the collection of Russell Sturgis, a New York architect, critic and writer.

Samuel Sherer, who in 1923 succeeded Robert Holland as director, ranged widely over the history of art in his buying for the Museum. Although American paintings continued to be added through purchase and gift, such as Charles F. Wimar's *The Captive Charger* (227), the gift of Miss Lillie B. Randell, Sherer tended to give a stronger emphasis to European art. He also began buying in the ancient field, acquiring Egyptian material and Greek and Roman sculpture as well as vases and small bronzes. Among his European purchases were several notable paintings such as the beautiful *Still Life* by Pieter Claesz (95) and a *Portrait of a Man with Gold Coins* (86), once catalogued as Franco-Flemish in origin, but given now by Professor Charles Sterling to Jean Clouet. In 1928 Cora Liggett Fowler bequeathed the Museum a number of paintings, among them *View in Suffolk* (135), an important early work by Thomas Gainsborough. Other paintings given in that year came from Mrs. Eugene A. Perry in memory of her mother, Mrs. Claude Kilpatrick. The Perry gifts included an especially appealing picture by Jacob Ochtervelt, *The Street Musicians* (101).

The late 1920s also saw the Museum receive approximately half the splendid collection of Near Eastern carpets formed over many years by James F. Ballard. The other half was given to The Metropolitan Museum of Art. Mr. Ballard's rugs gave the Museum strength in this area of collecting. In 1972 Mr. Ballard's daughter, Nellie Ballard White, added numerous fine rugs inherited from her father, thus further enhancing an already notable collection.

Throughout the 1920s the print collection continued to develop, especially through the interest of Horace M. Swope, who later served on the Board of Control. At that time Mr. Swope gave some of his old master prints and he continued to add to the Museum's collection throughout his life. The rest of the Swope collection, including many fine impressions from the 15th through the 19th century, was bequeathed to the Museum in 1939, the year of his death.

When Samuel Sherer died in 1928 he was succeeded as director by Meyric Rogers who came to St. Louis in October, 1929, from the directorship of The Baltimore Museum of Art. Rogers spent ten years in St. Louis before resigning to accept an appointment as curator of decorative and industrial arts at The Art Institute of Chicago. In his term of office Rogers followed the direction marked by his predecessors, that of continuing to broaden the collection generally; whenever possible, he acquired works of art of superb quality and the Museum is today indebted to him for his taste and good judgement. As American decorative art and architecture were of special interest to Meyric Rogers he began, soon after his arrival, to acquire fine quality American 18th century furniture for use in the period rooms which were on hand and awaiting installation on the lower level. Except for the Missouri Room, taken from the Nicholas Burckhartt house in Howard County, and not installed until 1943, the American rooms were open in 1930. A suite of four English rooms and one French room had been installed in 1929 on the west side of the main floor. It should be noted, however, that all the period rooms had to be adapted to the spaces assigned them.

Between 1933 and 1937 outstanding Impressionist and Post-Impressionist paintings were purchased, such as Pierre Auguste Renoir's portrait of his father (157); Georges Seurat's *Port-en-Bessin: The Outer Harbor (Low Tide)* (166); Eugène Boudin's charming small *Beach Scene* (155); Henri Fantin-Latour's *The Two Sisters* (154); and a superlative work by Vincent van Gogh, *Stairway at Auvers* (166), one of the finest acquisitions ever made by the Museum and now one of four paintings by the artist in its collection. Three 18th century French paintings were also acquired, Jean-Honoré Fragonard's *The Washerwomen* (128); François Boucher's *The Dovecote* (130); and Jean-Baptiste Siméon Chardin's *The Silver Goblet* (128). Nor were the old masters neglected, for in these years Lucas Cranach the Elder's beautifully preserved *The Judgement of Paris* (84) and Titian's *Christ Shown to the People* (74) were purchased, as well as Antonello Gagini's life-size marble sculpture of *St. Catherine of Alexandria* (69).

At the same time the Museum received an outstanding 16th century Flemish tapestry, *The Prophecy of Nathan* (83), a gift from Leicester Busch Faust and Audrey Faust Wallace, given in memory of their parents. In a quite different vein was the purchase of a major English period painting by John Singleton Copley, his portrait of *Henry Addington, First Viscount Sidmouth* (139). Notable, too, was the acquisition of the English and Continental 18th and 19th century miniatures collected over many years by Frank Spiekerman, a former St. Louisan. These were given in 1933 by Edna Louise Spiekerman as a memorial to her husband. Among the American pictures was *Raftsmen Playing Cards* (227), the Museum's first genre painting by George Caleb Bingham, an artist who was then far from achieving the national importance he has been so rightfully accorded in recent years. In the last years of Meyric Rogers' directorship the Museum purchased *Girl with Mandolin* (155), a painting of subtle beauty by Jean-Baptiste-Camille Corot; *The Mother* (172), an early work by Pablo Picasso which was the first painting by this master to enter the collections; and Marsden Hartley's *Smelt Brook Falls* (251). The latter was bought through the Eliza McMillan Fund which, not long after it was bequeathed in 1915, began to play an important role in the development of the Museum's collections, especially in reference to American art.

During Meyric Rogers' time the medieval section was begun. Although still small, it nevertheless includes a number of very fine objects acquired in the 1930s and later, typified by the mid-15th century limestone Burgundian sculpture of *St. Christopher* (59). One of the most distinguished acquisitions made during the Rogers years is the crucifixion lancet window (53), datable around 1200, from Montreuil-sur-Loire.

In these years the president of the Museum was Louis La Beaume, an architect and well-known St. Louisan who had succeeded to this office following William Bixby's death. The new president was interested in seeing the Museum acquire medieval architectural stonework. Unfortunately, the creation of a setting which would simulate a medieval chapel for the display of authentic material tended to violate the classic plan of Cass Gilbert's building. It marked the beginning of other architectural changes which appeared to be necessary at the time owing to the growth of the collections. These changes further disrupted the once orderly arrangement of the main floor. A change which had enhanced the appearance of the building was the laying in 1929 of a marble floor in Sculpture Hall, but this improvement was somewhat modified when the Roman brick walls were spray coated with a material which subtly interfered with the scale of this magnificent space.

Louis La Beaume was instrumental in purchasing the impressive early 16th century wooden staircase from Morlaix, a town in Brittany. So large an architectural unit inevitably presented a challenge in terms of its installation, but a solution was found by cutting off one end of one of the finest galleries that the Museum had for the display of paintings. So major an alteration demonstrated even then the serious lack of exhibition space for the Museum's growing collections. The problem could not be solved by tampering with the precise order which Cass Gilbert had originally given to the building. A positive physical change which helped to enlarge the available exhibition space was the removal in 1938 of the Richardson Memorial Library from the main floor galleries to new quarters on the lower level where it is situated today.

The public responded favorably to the many opportunities offered by their Art Museum and the *Annual Report* for 1938-39 reports an attendance of 390,000, a figure not surpassed until the great post-war exhibition of masterpieces from Berlin, when it reached 566,000. In recent years annual attendance at the Museum has averaged well above the half million mark and in 1969-70, the year of the second van Gogh exhibition, it reached 701,409. To knowledgeable visitors it was becoming ever more apparent that City Art Museum had to be counted among the principal art museums of the country. It was apparent, too, that its forward movement was inevitable, despite occasional difficult periods. The staff, trained and professional in outlook, recognized its responsibility to make the collections available and meaningful to the general public. Much attention, therefore, continued to be given to the department of education which was established in 1923.

The next director after Meyric Rogers was Perry Townsend Rathbone. Until he came to St. Louis in August, 1940, Rathbone had been curator of the Russell A. Alger Museum at Grosse Pointe Farms, Michigan. Louis La Beaume stepped down as president in 1941 and was followed by Daniel Catlin, who was to work closely with the newly appointed director in further developing the Museum. In 1940 the Chinese collection was greatly enriched when it was bequeathed an important part of Samuel C. Davis' collection of Chinese pottery and porcelain dating from the Han to the Ch'ing Dynasties. With the arrival of the Davis collection the Museum could at last show considerable strength in this area. Like Horace M. Swope, Samuel C. Davis had long maintained close ties with the Museum through his service on the Board of Control and his interest in collecting. Among other notable acquisitions in 1940-41 were Lyonel Feininger's well-known *The Glorious Victory of the Sloop Maria* (249) and the sensitive portrait of *Chester Harding Krum* (230), grandson of the artist, Chester Harding. At the same time the Museum bought *Venus with the Necklace* (185), the second of five casts of a major bronze by Aristide Maillol.

The Second World War brought far-reaching changes and in some ways marked the end of an era. The Museum lost some of its personnel to military service, including its director. Thus, from August 1943 to the fall of 1945, Charles Nagel, who had been a member of the Board from 1938 to 1942, acted on Rathbone's behalf. Under his leadership the Museum continued to make progress in a difficult period and to plan for the future. Hans Holbein the Younger's portrait of *Lady Guldeford* (87) had just been purchased; so, too, had Nicholas de Largillière's *Madame de la Martellière* (129), a work which extended the range of what was still a quite small collection of pre-19th century French painting. In these same years, Mrs. Jackson Johnson gave Thomas Gainsborough's full-length portrait of *Lords John and Bernard Stuart* (134), a fascinating and instructive picture after the van Dyck original owned by Earl Mountbatten of Burma. With the acquisition of this painting the Museum now had in its possession two outstanding and very different works by the artist.

Considering the general dislocation caused by the war years, it is surprising to note how many fine works of art entered the collections between about 1940 and 1945. The *Annual Report* for 1943-44 records the purchase of a major Florentine mannerist portrait of a young nobleman (73), a work which may not yet have been identified beyond question. Dating from the first half of the 16th century, the portrait has been given to both Francesco Salviati and Michele Tosini. The sitter has been tentatively identified as either Lorenzino de Medici or Alessandro de Medici. Still another significant acquisition was the Piero de Cosimo altarpiece, *Madonna and Child Enthroned with Saints* (65). In addition to these paintings the Museum also bought *St. Lawrence Distributing the Riches of the Church* (102), an outstanding work by the Genoese master, Bernardo Strozzi; *Mandolin and Vase of Flowers* (190), by Picasso; and a magnificent still life, *The Blue Mandolin* (191), by Georges Braque. These two 20th century paintings were soon joined by *At the Suresnes Ball* (171), an unusual and rare early large-scale painting by André Derain. The now famous *The Jolly Flatboatmen in Port* (226), by George Caleb Bingham, also came into the collection at this time.

Toward the end of 1945 Rathbone returned from military service and although Charles Nagel had accepted the Museum's newly created post of associate director, it was not long before he was asked to assume the directorship of the Brooklyn Museum. Under Rathbone's leadership, many outstanding exhibitions were brought to St. Louis, such as *Berlin Masterpieces, Vienna Treasures,* and *Paintings by Vincent van Gogh.* These and other exhibitions, especially *Mississippi Panorama,* which was organized by the director and his staff, stimulated public interest and pride in St. Louis' Art Museum. The times had changed and through exhibitions museums more than ever were attempting to reach out to capture the attention of new audiences.

In the nine post-war years of Perry Rathbone's directorship many works of art of outstanding quality entered the Museum. Though the purchase funds derived from tax income tended to be less than before the war, the Museum made the best possible use of them. In 1945-46 it managed to buy a superb cast of Auguste Rodin's *St. John the Baptist* (158); Giovanni Paolo Panini's *Interior of St. Peter's, Rome* (110); and a fine William M. Harnett still life (237). There was also an early interior painted at Nice by Henri Matisse (178), and a notable Max Beckmann, titled *Young Men by the Sea* (198). A gift of American silver was made at this time by Charles H. Stix, in memory of his mother, Mrs. Henry Stix. Of special importance in this small collection is the splendid coffee pot by the 18th century New York silversmith, Myer Myers (205). From 1946 to 1950 the parade of acquisitions continues. Acquired in those years were Winslow Homer's *The Country School* (234); Alexander Calder's *White Lily* (254); Giovanni Angelo Montorsoli's *Reclining Pan* (72), a Renaissance work of impressive quality; and an important Sung Dynasty sculpture of Kuan Yin (285).

American art, which to some extent the Museum had always collected, now began to assume greater significance owing to a number of important additions made toward the end of the 1940s. Several watercolors by Maurice Prendergast and Charles Demuth were purchased for the growing collection of drawings and watercolors; but more important was the acquisition of John Greenwood's *Sea Captains Carousing in Surinam* (208) and Ralph Earl's portraits of *Major Moses Seymour* (210) and *Mrs. Moses Seymour and her son, Epaphroditus* (210). The portraits of *Thaddeus Burr* (209) and *Eunice Dennie Burr* (209), by John Singleton Copley, complementing Ralph Earl's portraits, came a year or two later, as did Bingham's *The Wood Boat* (226). An especially fine landscape by John F. Kensett, a work titled *Upper Mississippi* (228), and therefore especially appropriate for St. Louis, was another welcome addition. These and other newly acquired pictures helped bring the American collections into sharper focus.

Among European works of art to appear between the late 1940s and the mid-1950s were many that added luster to the collections. From the famous sale of the collections formed over many years by Joseph H. Brummer, held at Parke Bernet in the spring of 1949, the Museum bought twenty-seven objects including a Romanesque capital from La Charité-sur-Loire and a remarkable early 12th century German brass crucifix figure (50). Nicolaes Maes' *The Housekeeper* (99) was purchased in these years as was the exquisite small triptych by Jan Provost (64). Over the next few years other notable works of art were acquired which raised the level of the Museum's collections as a whole. Among these was Rembrandt van Rijn's portrait of a young man (100) and a 6th century B.C. Greek bronze helmet (33).

Other interesting material acquired about this time contributed substance and variety to the collections, a group of 18th and 19th century Russian church vestments which came from Morton D. May, who was just then beginning to develop his now long-standing interest in the Museum, and an exceptional lacquer domed chest from 18th century Mexico (202), the gift

of Stratford Lee Morton. But of the utmost significance in these years was the gift by J. Lionberger Davis of his collection of thirty-five early Chinese bronzes. As in the case of Samuel C. Davis' bequest of Chinese ceramics in 1940, Lionberger Davis' bronzes added further depth to the Museum's representation of Far Eastern art. Because of his concern that the Museum's collections continue to improve in quality, this dedicated collector maintained his generosity almost to the end of his life, as witness his gift in 1954 of fifty fine Peruvian antiquities.

In April, 1952, the Friends of City Art Museum was founded, an organization designed to promote membership and to raise purchase funds for the enrichment of the collections. Through this invaluable organization the Museum has acquired an astonishing range of works of art which otherwise it would not have been able to purchase. Now consisting of thousands of St. Louisans, the Friends has made many significant contributions to the Museum as a whole. The first acquisition from the Friends fund was a Sumerian copper bull's head with lapis lazuli eyes, dating from about 2800-2600 B.C. (25).

The closer personal ties to the Museum which membership in the Friends affords has stimulated a far wider public interest in the collections. This interest has had the effect of encouraging many valuable gifts. While Lionberger Davis and Morton D. May continued their support, others, such as Louise and Joseph Pulitzer, Jr., began to strengthen the Museum with gifts from their collection. In 1952 Mr. Pulitzer gave a group of important watercolors, drawings and paintings, including Paul Klee's *The Man of Confusion* (195). Sydney M. Shoenberg, Sr., also began his lasting interest by adding a number of 18th century English pictures, among them a fine portrait by George Romney, and major gifts of important European paintings were made by Mrs. Mark C. Steinberg.

To the collection of decorative art which had been enjoying steady though unspectacular growth, was now added an important collection of textiles from the Greek isles and the eastern Mediterranean. The donor was Beatrice Lindell Cook, resident in England for many years though a former St. Louisan. A significant addition to what was still a modest representation of European porcelains was a figure of Augustus III of Saxony, modeled at Meissen by Johann Joachim Kändler (125). This superb object takes its place in the collection with other German and French porcelains including an equally important Meissen tea and coffee service (124).

During the latter phase of Mr. Rathbone's directorship several very fine pictures were purchased, such as the portrait of the *Comtesse de Valmont*, an early work by Jean François Millet (153), and an exquisite 17th century Dutch still life of flowers by Balthasar van der Ast (93). Still another important picture was Eugène Delacroix's *The Capture of Weislingen* (154), purchased through a bequest made by Mrs. Emelie Weindel. Through the interest of the Misses Effie and Stella Kuhn, a late 15th century marble relief of the *Adoration of the Shepherds* (66), by Giovanni Antonio Amadeo, was bought. From the estate of Curt Valentin the Museum was bequeathed an impressive Renoir bronze, *Venus Victorious* (177) and an early Max Beckmann, *Christ and the Woman Taken in Adultery* (183). Another important addition to the growing collection of 20th century art was Marc Chagall's *Temptation* (174), dating from 1911, a large-scale work which shows his awareness of Cubism.

By the early 1950s the City Art Museum building was fifty years old. It was beginning to show age and to be less adaptable to use. Both Nagel and Rathbone had more than once in their annual reports called attention to the physical needs of the building, reminding St. Louisans that if they were to have a great Museum — a goal nearly at hand — then a setting worthy of the collections was essential. Space to exhibit the collections was of the utmost importance; so too were work and storage areas almost totally lacking in the original building. Plans for a restaurant and education wing featuring an auditorium were under discussion even before the war. It was not until 1954, however, that the restaurant was built; the education wing and auditorium were not ready until 1959.

In May, 1955, Perry Rathbone resigned to accept the directorship of the Museum of Fine Arts, Boston. He was succeeded by Charles Nagel, the Museum's former associate director who returned to St. Louis from his post as director of The Brooklyn Museum. Nagel was to hold the St. Louis directorship until his retirement in the summer of 1964. A highly important acquisition early in Mr. Nagel's time was the purchase of a female portrait by Frans Hals (96). This distinguished picture greatly enhanced the Museum's small collection of 17th century Dutch painting just as the Rembrandt portrait had done a few years earlier. The painting by Hals was followed by Jacob Jordaens' *Suffer the Children to Come Unto Me* (94), considered to be among the finest pictures by this master in an American collection. An acquisition of a very different order was that of a Peruvian mantle, accompanied by a matching turban, shirt and poncho (352). This strikingly beautiful textile dating from the 5th to the 2nd century B.C. was bought with Friends funds with assistance from Maymar Corporation through Mr. and Mrs. Samuel A. Marx.

Many other gifts were made in the late 1950s by collectors and patrons of the Museum. From Charles E. and Mary Merrill came a 1924 painting, *Dark Abstraction* (249), by Georgia O'Keeffe, the first work by the artist to enter the collection. Mr. and Mrs. Morton D. May gave paintings by Karl Knaths and Marsden Hartley as well as a large group of German Expressionist watercolors and drawings. They also added several fine 20th century sculptures to their already numerous gifts; an impressive mid-twenties bronze Cubist figure called *The Bather* (180), by Jacques Lipchitz; *Horse and Rider* (199), a bronze by Marino

Marini; and an abstract marble sculpture by Henry Moore. It was also at this time that Mr. and Mrs. May began to give fine examples of sculpture from Central Africa.

Through Mrs. Steinberg's continuing interest in the Museum, a large Monet waterlily subject was acquired (163). This fine picture was purchased through the Steinberg Charitable Fund. From her own collection, Mrs. Steinberg gave the bronze *Ballet Dancer* (160), by Edgar Degas. With gifts of this quality the Museum's late 19th-early 20th century collection was obviously becoming increasingly important. Within a year, further interest was added to it when Mr. and Mrs. Richard K. Weil contributed *Decorative Figure* (172), a superb Matisse bronze, one of the first of a number of important gifts from this outstanding St. Louis private collection.

A further strengthening of the 20th century collection resulted when Louise and Joseph Pulitzer Jr., gave *Masquerade* (198), an important early painting by Max Beckmann. Also during the 1950s these generous donors gave their cast of Jacques Lipchitz' *Figure* (189), a large and compellingly mysterious bronze sculpture which presents a strikingly different aspect of the artist's personality from that seen in Morton May's *Bather*. Two other outstanding paintings now came from Mrs. Steinberg: *The Hüth Factories at Clichy* (165), by van Gogh, and Paul Gauguin's portrait of *Madame Roulin* (164). From Martha I. Love the Museum received a work of art of a very different kind, an impressive 2nd century portrait from Palmyra (46), carved in marble in high relief. All through the 1950s the print collection continued to grow, largely because of gifts made to it as there were no funds reserved for this purpose alone. The principal donors at this time were Moyer S. Fleisher, Henry V. Putzel and Borden S. Veeder.

As the 1950s came to an end it was apparent that the Museum's general purchase funds, derived through the mill tax, were approaching low ebb.

At best they had never been substantial, yet now they amounted to less than ever before. For fifty years the rate had remained unchanged while the cost of operating the Museum was increasing year by year. With the dramatic rise in the cost of works of art, so clearly evident by the early 1960s, the Museum was hard pressed to reserve tax money for its collections. An important change in the Museum came about in 1959 when the auditorium was built, together with space for the department of education and the Friends. The auditorium has ever since been a prime asset, frequently utilized to capacity.

Daniel Catlin, president of the Board of Control since 1940, and instrumental in activating many changes in the Museum, including the building of the auditorium, resigned in 1960. He was succeeded by Henry B. Pflager who continued his predecessor's interest in improving the building. In 1961 renovation work was started on a number of west side galleries for special exhibitions use. In the process a spacious second floor area was built for the display of the now extensive collection of American paintings. A major accomplishment during the latter part of Charles Nagel's directorship was the establishment of a department of conservation. With a conservator now on the staff more rigorous standards could be applied to the collections and immediate attention could be given to their preservation.

Early in 1962 St. Louis voters authorized a doubling of the mill tax rate, a welcome and long overdue move which provided relief from immediate financial pressures. Unfortunately, the increase was far from being enough to allow the Museum to look beyond its most urgent concerns to a reasonably secure future. This was to become increasingly apparent over the next decade.

At the time this handbook introduction is being written the sixth director is in his eleventh year. Charles Edward Buckley became director on November 1, 1964. Previously he had been director of The Currier Gallery of Art, Manchester, New Hampshire. Over the next few years the St. Louis staff was to be enlarged, particularly in the curatorial department. At present the Museum has five associate curators and one curatorial assistant.

Collecting over the last ten years has continued along the same lines as in the past, and both European and American paintings, sculpture, prints and drawings have been acquired. The Far East and the decorative arts fields have received particular attention, and in recent years, especially owing to the interest of Morton D. May, far more consideration has been given to the primitive arts, particularly Pre-Columbian material.

Among the acquisitions of European painting only a few can be mentioned. For example, the pair of portraits of Mr. and Mrs. Robert Gwillym (137), by Joseph Wright of Derby, bought for the Museum by Miss Martha I. Love in memory of Daniel Catlin; the pair of oil studies by Luca Giordano (108), which are closely connected with his last major work in Naples; an *Interior Scene with Peasants Dancing* (99), by Adriaen van Ostade; a view over the estuary of the Maas, near Dordrecht, an early and important work by Aelbert Cuyp (98); and the splendid portrait of Cardinal Jean de Rochechouart (114), by Pompeo Girolamo Batoni. Except for the paintings by Wright these paintings were bought with Friends funds. Toward the end of 1974 the Edward Mallinckrodt bequest introduced into the collection a number of good Barbizon School pictures and George Romney's *Portrait of a Lady* (136).

In 1965 two highly important 20th century paintings, *Bathers with a Turtle* (173), by Henri Matisse, and *Standing Nude* (181), by Joan Miró, were acquired. The Matisse, from 1908, is one of the finest pictures by this master in an American collection and is a gift from Louise and Joseph Pulitzer, Jr. Miró's *Standing Nude*, painted in 1918, can be said to have somewhat

the same relation to the early work of that artist as does *Bathers with a Turtle* to that of Matisse. The purchase of the Miró was made from the Friends fund, as was another outstanding 20th century work, Alberto Giacometti's bronze, *Hands Holding the Void* (194), from 1934-35, and Piet Mondrian's *Composition of Red and White* (196), painted in 1938-42.

The last decade has seen many other fine 20th century paintings and sculptures enter the Museum's collection in addition to the ones already mentioned. Mr. Pulitzer has continued his benefactions by giving *Elvira Resting at a Table* (178), by Amedeo Modigliani. The painting was given in memory of his late wife, Louise Vauclain Pulitzer. Also from Mr. Pulitzer came *The Fireplace* (179), painted by Picasso in 1916-17. In the light of the quality and number of the Pulitzer gifts over the last fifteen years it would be difficult to overstate their importance.

Other impressive gifts which have added immeasurably to the Museum's representation of Impressionist and Post Impressionist painting have come from Sydney M. Shoenberg, Sr. For example, in 1972 the Museum received a brilliant van Gogh, *Still Life with Apples* (165), dating from 1887 when the artist was in Paris. In the following year Mr. Shoenberg gave *The Railroad Bridge at Argenteuil* (162), painted by Monet between 1875-77.

As the American collection is one of the Museum's strengths, pictures of excellent quality have been consistently added to it over the better part of a decade. In 1968 John Allan Love made possible the purchase of *The Hudson at Piermont* (229), a large and distinguished work by Jasper Francis Cropsey, and in 1969, *Woodland Landscape* (230), by Asher Brown Durand. Both paintings were acquired in memory of his late wife Mary Potter Love. Among other 19th century American pictures which are relatively new in the collection are *Rumford Point, Maine* (235) by Harrison B. Brown, a landscape evocative of small town northern New England life, given by Mr. and Mrs. Warren McK. Shapleigh and Mrs. Arthur Hoskins; a beautiful landscape from the late 1830s by Thomas Cole (218), a work which entered the collection by exchange and by purchase through the Friends fund and the Eliza McMillan Trust Fund; and two fine paintings by Martin Johnson Heade, both from 1863, *A Vase of Corn Lilies and Heliotrope* (230) and a view over the saltmarsh meadows near Newburyport, Massachusetts. Ever since 1913, the American collections have grown, sometimes slowly and sometimes more rapidly as they have in recent years.

Since about 1965 a number of contemporary American paintings and sculpture also have been acquired. In 1967 Mr. and Mrs. Norman B. Champ, Jr., gave funds for the purchase of a major sculpture, *Praise for Elohim Adonai* (265), by Mark di Suvero. Through the interest of Mr. and Mrs. Joseph A. Helman and Mr. and Mrs. Ronald K. Greenberg, and with help from the Friends, the Museum was fortunate in acquiring *Marriage of Reason and Squalor* (257), a 1959 work by Frank Stella. From the Shoenberg Foundation, Inc., came *Red, Orange, Orange on Red* (259), by Mark Rothko; *Alpha-Tau* (260), a large painting by Morris Louis; and *Giant 3-Way Plug "Cube Tap"* (264), the second of three casts authorized by the sculptor, Claes Oldenburg. To these works were added other large scale paintings by Tom Holland, Peter Young, Ron Davis and Bruce Nauman. Here the Contemporary Art Society, established in 1968, has played an impressive role in providing funds or in stimulating gifts. In the case of the Davis and the Nauman, assistance for their purchase was provided by a grant from the National Endowment for the Arts. At about the same time the Museum added *Young Woman in Green* (244), painted in 1915 by William Glackens and given by the artist's son and daughter-in-law, Ira and Nancy Glackens; *Gas House District* (250), by Niles Spencer, a gift from Marie and G. Gordon Hertslet with the addition of Museum funds; and *Out the*

Window (251), by Arthur G. Dove, purchased with Museum funds.

Other works of art which have helped to round out the American collection came from the estate of Marie Setz Hertslet, who bequeathed a number of beautiful and important early 20th century American paintings, such as *Boathouse, Winter, Harlem River* (246), by Ernest Lawson; and *Houston Street* (245), by George Luks, as well as watercolors and drawings by Childe Hassam, John Sloan, John Marin and Charles Sheeler. In 1971 the Museum was fortunate in adding twenty-four superb watercolors by Seth Eastman from a recently rediscovered album which had once belonged to the artist, Henry Lewis. A number of St. Louis collectors and two St. Louis firms, Lafayette Federal and the St. Louis headquarters of Western Electric helped make possible these acquisitions.

In the field of drawings and prints, whether American or European, the acquisitions are too numerous to mention, although one cannot overlook the importance of the large group of 20th century prints, mostly by the new generation of American printmakers, which was built up in the late 1960s and early 1970s with funds provided by Sadie and Sidney S. Cohen. The Cohen gifts have given the Museum a definite strength in this area which was all but lacking before they began to help the Museum. Subsequently, the Cohens provided funds for numerous 17th century Italian prints, once again developing a side of the collection which had formerly received only modest attention.

Several other works also merit special mention, Jacques Villon's superb drawing of his father (176), given by Mr. and Mrs. George S. Rosborough, Jr., and The Measuregraph Company; and several 18th and 19th century English watercolors and drawings, including John Hamilton Mortimer's *Banditti Regaling* (140), given by Mr. and Mrs. Christian B. Peper.

Through the Decorative Arts Society, founded in 1967, the Museum has been able to make numerous purchases and has also received many gifts. Some excellent 19th century furniture has been acquired, such as the outstanding sofa table (222), by Anthony G. Quervelle, which was given by Mr. and Mrs. Sanford N. McDonnell in honor of Mr. and Mrs. William A. McDonnell; a library table in the Renaissance revival taste (221), by the New York cabinetmaker, Alexander Roux; and a pair of stained glass windows (233), designed by John LaFarge for the Frederick Lothrop Ames house in Boston, the last two purchased with funds from the Society. In 1972 Mrs. William A. McDonnell's gift of twenty-nine 17th to early 19th century English and Continental embroidered pictures enhanced the Museum's collection. Since they were founded, both the Contemporary Art Society and the Decorative Arts Society have had a strong influence on the collections in their respective areas of interest.

In Far Eastern art many additions to the collection have been made since about 1965. Through the interest of Helen and Arthur B. Baer several notable Japanese objects were purchased, such as the Ao-Kutani plate (312); a Ko-Imari jar of splendid quality (311); and a pair of six-fold early Edo Period screens of the Kano School (314-15). These gifts from the Baers have vastly strengthened our still small collection of Japanese art. To this same collection funds from the Mary Ranken Jordan and Ettie A. Jordan Charitable Foundation added a very fine early 18th century Nabeshima ware ewer (312), while other Japanese porcelains came to us through the Friends.

The Jordan Foundation also provided a fine Kamakura Period figure of *Fudo-Myōō* (308), from the first half of the 13th century while the Bixby Fund has been used to develop the Japanese collection as well as our representation of Indian sculpture. In the latter field Bixby funds have provided a very fine seated *Vajrasattva* (323) of 7th to 8th century Nepalese origin and a bronze 12th to 14th century *Skanda-Karttikeya* (323), also from Nepal. A third sculpture, an 11th century Indian bronze figure of *Parvati* (321), was purchased with funds given by the Charles E. Merrill Trust.

The last ten years have seen the collections grow in many directions, although basically with the idea of strengthening areas where the Museum was already well developed. An essential and too long deferred task now lies ahead, that of providing the proper care, display and interpretation of its extensive collections. New galleries are urgently required, especially to accommodate the primitive materials already owned and those much larger and more important collections from Middle and South America, Central Africa, the South Pacific and the Pacific Northwest, which are on loan from Mr. and Mrs. Morton D. May, and which over the next few years may well become a part of the Museum's permanent collections.

Since 1971 the Museum has been studying its building with the help of its architects, Hardy Holzman Pfeiffer Associates, New York. As a result of their in-depth study a long-range plan has been prepared. The first step toward a new future for the Museum was taken in the spring of 1975 when extensive renovation work began in approximately two-thirds of the Cass Gilbert building. Beyond these changes, which will be far-reaching, others involving new construction are contemplated. It is hoped by the Museum's many friends that in the not too distant future many of the current problems relating to the building will be solved to the satisfaction of the large community now served by this venerable institution.

Charles E. Buckley
June 30, 1975

ILLUSTRATIONS

PORTRAIT OF AN OFFICIAL
Old Kingdom, 2680-2258 B.C.
Porphyritic granite, Height: 54.6 cm.
Purchase: Friends Fund   51:1956

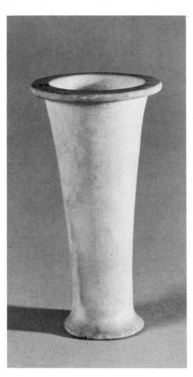

OINTMENT JAR
Middle Kingdom, ca. 2000 B.C.
Alabaster, Height: 17.0 cm.
Purchase 142:1921

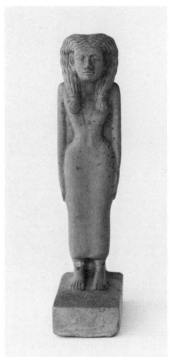

FIGURE OF A WOMAN
12th Dynasty, 1991-1786 B.C.
Limestone, Height: 16.5 cm.
Purchase 30:1924

BOWL, Early Dynastic, 3200-2680 B.C., Green slate, Diameter: 24.3 cm., Purchase 26:1924

MARRIAGE SCARAB OF KING AMENHOTEP III
AND QUEEN TIY
18th Dynasty, 1570-1314 B.C.
Steatite, Height: 10.3 cm.
Purchase 193:1924

STEM CUP
18th Dynasty, 1494-1479 B.C.
Gold, Height: 9.1 cm.
Purchase: Friends Fund 51:1959

NECKLACE COUNTERWEIGHT
18th Dynasty, 1570-1314 B.C.
Bronze, Height: 7.0 cm.
Purchase 35:1924

BOTTLE
18th Dynasty, 1570-1314 B.C.
Glazed earthenware, Height: 14.9 cm.
Gift of the Bachstitz Gallery 177:1925

HEAD OF AN AFRICAN PRISONER, 18th Dynasty, ca. 1370 B.C., Limestone, Width: 24.8 cm. Purchase 18:1940

PILGRIM BOTTLE
26th Dynasty, 663-525 B.C.
Glazed earthenware, Height: 15.1 cm.
Purchase 199:1924

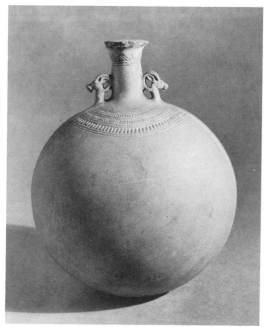

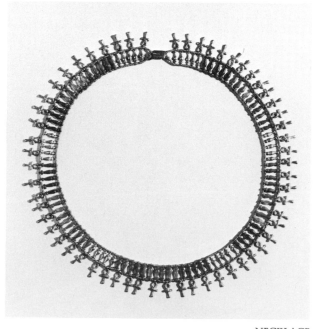

NECKLACE
18th Dynasty, 1570-1314 B.C.
Gold, lapis lazuli, cornelian, feldspar
Length: 45.7 cm. Purchase 16:1940

THREE SCENES FROM THE TOMB OF PRINCE MENTUEMHAT, 26th Dynasty, 663-525 B.C., Limestone, Length: 165.5 cm. Purchase 1:1958

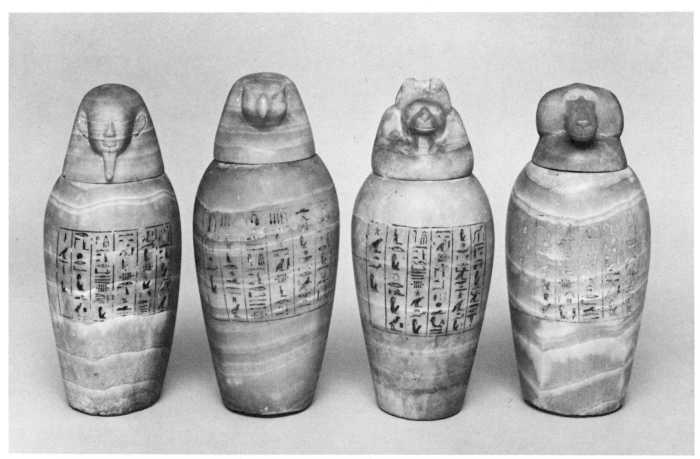

CANOPIC JARS, 19th-20th Dynasties, 1314-1085 B.C., Alabaster, Heights: 40.6 cm. Purchase 210-213:1924

ANKH-PA-KHERED WITH OSIRIS
26th Dynasty, 655-640 B.C.
Green-black schist, Height: 41.3 cm.
Purchase 222:1924

NEFER-ATMU OR NEFERTUM
26th Dynasty, 663-525 B.C.
Silver, Height: 24.8 cm.
Purchase 223:1924

CAT
26th-30th Dynasties, 663-341 B.C.
Bronze, Height: 19.7 cm.
Gift of Miss Cornelia Scott   24:1939

NECKLACE WITH THE GOD NEFERTUM
Ptolemaic Period, 332-30 B.C.
Gold, Figure Height: 4.9 cm.
Purchase 219:1924

Opposite
HEAD OF A BULL
Mesopotamian, Sumer, ca. 2800-2600 B.C.
Copper, shell and lapis lazuli
Height: 23.5 cm.
Purchase: Friends Fund   260:1951

BEARDED VOTIVE FIGURE
Lebanese, Jezzine, ca. 1500 B.C.
Copper, Height: 39.6 cm.
Purchase: Friends Fund   356:1958

HORSE BIT AND CHEEK PIECES
Iranian, Luristan, ca. 1000 B.C.
Bronze, Height: 17.8 cm.
Purchase 46:1931

DAGGER, Iranian, Luristan, 1085-1062 B.C., Bronze, Length: 42.3 cm. Gift of Joseph Ternbach 11-1964

SITULA
Iranian, Neo-Elamite Period, 9th century B.C.
Bronze, Height: 13.1 cm.
Gift of J. Lionberger Davis   231:1955

HORSE'S CHEEK PIECE
Iranian, Luristan, ca. 1000 B.C.
Bronze, Height: 13.0 cm.
Gift of J. Lionberger Davis   234:1955

RITUAL AXE-ADZE
Iranian, Luristan, 900-700 B.C.
Bronze, Width: 20.3 cm.
Gift of J. Lionberger Davis
102:1965

PIN WITH FABULOUS BEASTS IN COMBAT
Iranian, Luristan, 6th century B.C.
Bronze, Length: 16.9 cm.
Gift of J. Lionberger Davis   101:1965

FRAGMENT OF A PLAQUE
Part of the Ziwiyeh Treasure
Iranian, Kurdistan, 7th century B.C.
Gold, 6.7 x 13.0 cm.
Gift of J. Lionberger Davis   242:1955

GENIUS,
FROM THE THRONE OF SARGON II
Mesopotamian, Assyrian Period
Reign of Sargon II, 722-705 B.C.
Ivory, Height: 18.4 cm.
Purchase 33:1924

RELIEF OF A GENIUS FROM THE
NORTHWEST PALACE OF NIMRUD
Mesopotamian, Assyrian Period
Reign of Ashurnazirpal II, 885-859 B.C.
Alabaster, Height: 151.1 cm.
Purchase 186:1925

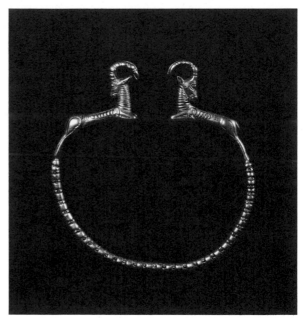

BRACELET
Iranian, Achaemenid Period
Late 6th-early 5th century B.C.
Gold, Height: 9.5 cm.
Anonymous Gift   121:1952

FRAGMENT OF A RELIEF: MAN WITH A KID
Iranian, Persepolis, Achaemenid Period,
Reign of Artaxerxes III, 359-338 B.C.
Limestone, Height: 49.7 cm.
Purchase 93:1954

BOWL
Iranian, Achaemenid Period
6th century B.C.
Silver, Diameter: 13.8 cm.
Purchase 174:1925

STEM CUP OF THE ZYGOURIES TYPE
Mycenaean, ca. 1275 B.C.
Earthenware, Height: 19.0 cm.
Purchase 283:1952

TWO FEMALE FIGURINES AND A BULL
Mycenaean, ca. 1300-1200 B.C.
Earthenware, Height of tallest: 11.8 cm.
Purchase 116, 117, 115:1951

OINOCHOE
Coastal Anatolian, ca. 625-590 B.C.
Earthenware, Height: 27.5 cm.
Purchase: Funds given by Miss Leona J. Beckmann
6:1965

FLAT-BOTTOMED OINOCHOE
Attributed to The Painter of the Dodwell Pyxis
Middle Corinthian, ca. 600-575 B.C.
Earthenware, Height: 15.9 cm.
Purchase 5:1927

PYXIS
Attributed to The Painter of the Dodwell Pyxis
Middle Corinthian, ca. 600-575 B.C.
Earthenware, Height: 16.5 cm.
Purchase 174:1924

CHALCIDIAN HELMET
Crest partially reconstructed
Ca. 550-500 B.C.
Bronze, silver and ivory inlay
Height: 72.0 cm.
Purchase 282:1949

Opposite
NECK AMPHORA:
SCENE OF FIGHTING
WITH WOMEN WATCHING
Attic, ca. 575-550 B.C.
Black-figure ware, Tyrrhenian group
Height: 39.1 cm.
Purchase 13:1926

HYDRIA
Corinthian, ca. 550-500 B.C.
Bronze, Height: 42.6 cm.
Purchase 169:1924

NECK AMPHORA: VICTORY WITH LYRE
Attributed to The Berlin Painter
Attic, ca. 490 B.C.
Red-figure ware, Height: 35.9 cm.
Purchase 57:1955

AMPHORA: COMBAT OF HERAKLES AND
APOLLO FOR THE DELPHIC TRIPOD
Attributed to The Antimenes Painter
Attic, ca. 530 B.C.
Black-figure ware, Height: 38.8 cm.
Purchase 39:1921

STAMNOS: DANCING MAENADS
Attributed to The Chicago Painter
Attic, ca. 490 B.C.
Red-figure ware, Height: 37.8 cm.
Bequest of Imogene Evans   15:1951

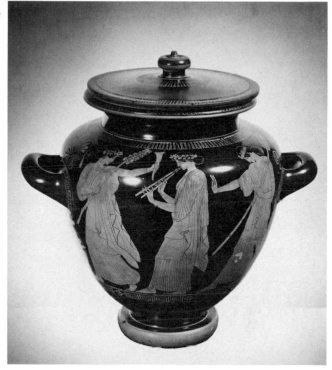

PITCHER
Corinthian, 4th century B.C.
Bronze, Height: 36.5 cm.
Purchase 29:1922

CALYX KRATER:
TRIPTOLEMOS AND DEMETER
The Marlay Painter
Attic, ca. 430 B.C.
Red-figure ware, Height: 31.8 cm.
Purchase 2:1929

HEAD OF A WOMAN FROM A GRAVE STATUE
Attic, ca. 350 B.C.
Parian marble, Height: 39.4 cm.
Purchase 57:1941

GRAVE STELE OF KALLISTRATA
Attic, ca. 400 B.C.
Marble, Height: 83.0 cm.
Purchase 4:1933

HEAD OF A BULL
Greek or Graeco-Roman
2nd-1st century B.C.
Marble, Height: 22.9 cm.
Purchase 1:1934

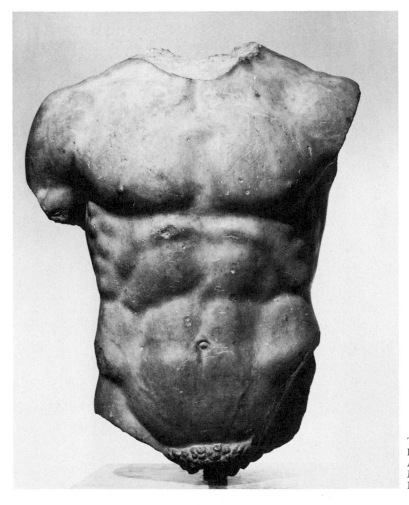

TORSO
Italy?, Roman, 1st century B.C.
After a 5th century B.C. Greek prototype
Marble, Height: 74.0 cm.
Purchase 6:1937

Opposite
ARTEMIS COLONNA
Hellenistic, Pergamum, 1st century B.C.?
After a 4th century B.C. prototype
Marble, Height: 142.3 cm.
Purchase 2:1934

ARTEMIS
Italy?, Roman, 2nd century B.C.
After early 4th century Greek prototype
Marble, Height: 73.0 cm.
Purchase 41:1924

THE INFANT HERAKLES
Hellenistic, 1st century B.C.
Bronze with silver inlay, Height: 62.3 cm.
Purchase 36:1926

DISK, PART OF BODY ARMOR
Etruscan, late 7th-6th century B.C.
Bronze, Diameter: 30.5 cm.
Purchase 51:1922

DISK, PART OF BODY ARMOR
Etruscan, late 7th-6th century B.C.
Bronze, Diameter: 22.8 cm.
Purchase 53:1922

TRIPOD
Etruscan, ca. 530-510 B.C.
Bronze, Height: 61.3 cm.
Purchase 37:1926

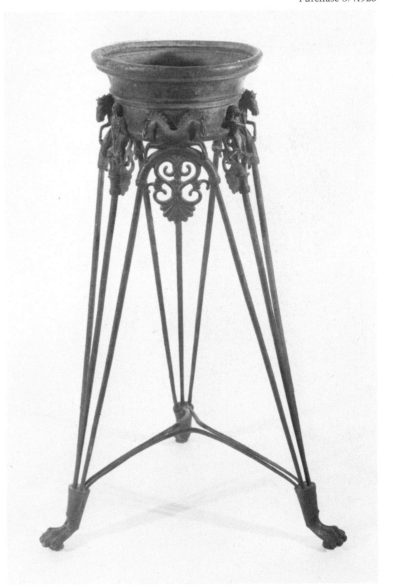

DISK, PART OF BODY ARMOR
Etruscan, late 7th-6th century B.C.
Bronze, Diameter: 20.3 cm.
Purchase 52:1922

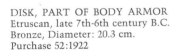

STEM CUP
Found in Syria, Roman, 1st century
Molded glass, Height: 11.2 cm.
Gift of Mrs. F. H. Cook   247:1952

ARRETINE MOLD
Stamp of Nicephorus Perennius
Roman, ca. 30-20 B.C.
Earthenware, Diameter: 19.5 cm.
Purchase 175:1925

MUG
Roman, ca. 100 B.C.-A.D. 100
Green glazed earthenware, Height: 15.2 cm.
Purchase 386:1923

Opposite
DETAIL FROM THE
CALYX KRATER
The Marlay Painter   2:1929
See page 35

HANDLE OF A SITULA
Roman, 1st century B.C.
Bronze, Length: 22.6 cm.
Purchase 148:1922

DANCING MAENAD
Syria?, Roman, 1st century
Bronze, Height: 22.0 cm.
Gift of J. Lionberger Davis   203:1954

PORTRAIT OF A PRIEST
Italy?, Roman, first half 1st century
Marble, Height: 26.7 cm.
Purchase 7:1922

PRINCE PARIS WATCHING
HIS FLOCK
ON MOUNT IDA
Roman, 1st century
Marble, Height: 34.0 cm.
Purchase 75:1942

PLATTER
Gallo-Roman, 3rd century
Silver and bronze, Diameter: 37.5 cm.
Purchase 11:1928

VOTIVE HAND
Roman, 3rd-4th century
Bronze, Height: 20.5 cm.
Purchase 52:1956

THE PRIEST YEDI BEL, 139-140, Syria, Palmyra, Marble, Height: 50.5 cm., Purchase: Funds given by Miss Martha I. Love   24:1960

BRACELET
Probably Egypt, Alexandria, 3rd-4th century
Gold, Diameter: 10.5 cm.
Purchase 54:1924

COVERED BOX
Byzantine, 5th-6th century(?)
Silver, Height: 8.7 cm.
Purchase 44:1924

VASE
Egypt, Coptic, 1st-3rd century(?)
Faience, Height: 23.3 cm.
Purchase 21:1928

TUNIC
Egypt, Coptic, 6th century
Linen and wool tapestry, Height: 109.4 cm.
Gift of The Olsen Foundation   70:1953

SECTION FROM A MOSAIC PAVEMENT
Syria, Antioch, 5th century
Marble, Length: 213.4 cm.
Purchase 742:1940

PORTRAIT OF A WOMAN
Egypt, Fayum, 4th century
Tempera on wood, 26.8 x 17.3 cm.
Gift of Mrs. Max A. Goldstein   128:1951

FRAGMENT OF A TUNIC
Egypt, Akhmin, Coptic, 4th-5th century
Linen and wool tapestry, 33.7 x 34.3 cm.
Purchase 48:1939

CRUCIFIX
Workshop of Rogerus of Helmarshausen
German, Hildesheim?, ca. 1130
Bronze dinanderie, Height: 17.8 cm.
Purchase 73:1949

INITIAL P
French, ca. 1100-1110
Tempera on parchment, 29.4 x 15.1 cm.
Purchase: Funds given by Daniel K. Catlin   63:1952

ELDER OF THE APOCALYPSE
Fragment of an archivolt
Western France, ca. 1150-70
Stone, Height: 46.7 cm.
Purchase 33:1933

MADONNA AND CHILD
French, Auvergne, 12th century
Polychromed wood, Height: 90.3 cm.
Purchase: Friends Fund   279:1952

ADORATION OF THE MAGI
German, last quarter of 12th century
Champlevé enamel and gilded copper, 11.8 x 12.9 cm.
Purchase 77:1949

CHASSE
French, Limoges, 2nd half 13th century
Champlevé enamel and gilded copper, Height: 12.9 cm.
Purchase 56:1949

FRAGMENT OF A VESTMENT
OF ABBOT ARNOLDO RAMON DE BUIRE
Spanish, Burgos, mid-13th century
Tabby weave, 31.4 x 24.7 cm.
Purchase 116:1952

STAINED GLASS WINDOW
French, Montreuil-sur-Loire, ca. 1200
Height: 259.2 cm.
Purchase 3:1935

Detail of 3:1935

A SEATED FIGURE
The Priest Melchizedek?
French, School of Rheims, early 13th century
Stained glass window, Height: 193.0 cm.
Purchase 137:1920

APOCALYPTIC SCENE
Italian, Padua, late 13th century
Tempera and gold leaf on parchment
17.4 x 12.1 cm.
Purchase 117:1952

FRAGMENT OF A SADDLE BOW
Spanish, 13th-14th century
Ivory, Length: 17.2 cm.
Purchase 34:1927

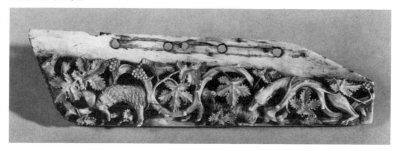

TEXTILE FRAGMENT
Italian, Sicilian(?), ca. 13th-14th century
Brocade, Length: 81.3 cm.
Purchase 19:1922

MADONNA AND CHILD WITH SAINTS
"The Sterbini Triptych"
Circle of Andrea Orcagna
Italian, Florence, mid-14th century
Tempera on panel, 40.6 x 44.5 cm.
Purchase 51:1926

ST. JOHN THE BAPTIST PREACHING
Fragment
The Master of San Torpè
Italian, Pisa-Siena, active ca. 1300
Tempera on panel, 58.6 x 63.5 cm.
Purchase 46:1941

MADONNA AND CHILD
French, Ile-de-France, 14th century
Limestone, Height: 188.0 cm.
Purchase 2:1930

A BISHOP SAINT
French, 14th century
Caen stone, Height: 195.9 cm.
Purchase 87:1949

MADONNA AND CHILD
French, Ile-de-France, 14th century
Ivory, Height: 18.6 cm.
Purchase 17:1926

MADONNA AND CHILD ENTHRONED
Spinello Aretino
Italian, Florence, ca. 1346-1410
Tempera on panel, 139.7 x 63.5 cm.
Purchase 48:1927

SCENES FROM THE PASSION OF CHRIST
French, Ile-de-France, late 14th century
Dyptich, Ivory, Height: 20.3 cm.
Purchase 183:1928

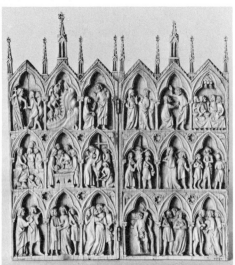

COFFER
French, 15th century
Wrought iron, Height: 11.4 cm.
Purchase 19:1919

PLATE
Hispano-Moresque, 15th century
Lead-glazed earthenware, Diameter: 46.4 cm.
Purchase 27:1932

THE CRUCIFIXION
Orphrey from a Chasuble
French, early 15th century
Linen, silk and gold embroidery
Height: 105.4 cm.
Purchase 76:1949

ST. CHRISTOPHER, French, Burgundy, ca. 1450, Limestone, Height: 78.7 cm. Purchase 3:1934

SALLET
German, late 15th century
Steel, Height: 24.4 cm.
Purchase 58:1939

URN
Flemish, ca. 1450
Bronze, Height: 41.0 cm.
Purchase 55:1949

"HUNGARIAN" SHIELD
Arms of the Tänzl of Tratzberg
German, late 15th century
Painted wood, Height: 68.3 cm.
Purchase 88:1942

Preceding page, detail from CHASUBLE *below*

RELIQUARY
German, late 15th century
Silver gilt, Height: 44.2 cm.
Purchase 101:1926

CHASUBLE WITH ORPHREYS
Spanish, possibly Toledo
Late 15th century
Embroidered silk and linen
Height: 162.6 cm.
Purchase 206:1916

CHRIST HEALING THE DEAF AND DUMB
Simon Bening, Flemish, 1483/4-1561
Tempera and gold leaf on parchment, 6.6 x 8.3 cm.
Purchase 66:1952

THE ANNUNCIATION
Gerard David
Flemish, ca. 1450-1523
Oil on panel, Diameter: 27.9 cm.
Purchase 204:1942

THE ENTOMBMENT
The Master of the Virgo inter Virgines
Dutch, active 1470-95
Oil on panel, 58.4 x 46.4 cm.
Purchase 4:1935

ST. MICHAEL FIGHTING THE DRAGON, 1498
Albrecht Dürer, German, 1471-1528
Woodcut, 40.7 x 29.2 cm.
Gift of Miss Berenice C. Ballard   843:1940

MADONNA AND CHILD
Italian, The Marches?, last quarter 15th century
Oil on panel, 42.5 x 27.7 cm.
Purchase 45:1927

ST. THOMAS AQUINAS CONFOUNDING AVERROES
Giovanni di Paolo
Italian, Siena, 1403-1483
Tempera on panel, 24.8 x 25.9 cm.
Purchase 56:1941

THE FLAGELLATION, THE CRUCIFIXION, THE DEPOSITION
Jan Provost, Flemish, ca. 1465-1529
Oil on panel, each: 27.3 x 21.0 cm.
Purchase 73, 74, 75:1950

MADONNA AND CHILD ENTHRONED WITH FOUR SAINTS, "The Pugliese Altar", Piero di Cosimo
Italian, Florence, 1462-1521, Tempera with oil glazes on panel, central panel: 166.4 x 113.0 cm., Purchase 1:1940

MARSYAS
Italian, Florence, late 15th century
Bronze, Height: 30.8 cm.
Purchase 153:1924

THE ADORATION OF THE SHEPHERDS
Giovanni Antonio Amadeo
Italian, Lombardy, 1447-1522
Marble, Height: 90.8 cm.
Gift of Effie and Stella Kuhn   60:1953

MADONNA AND CHILD WITH
STS. LOUIS OF TOULOUSE,
JOHN THE EVANGELIST
AND DONORS, 1486
The Master of the St. Louis Madonna
Italian, Florence, last quarter 15th century
Oil on panel, 151.2 x 80.0 cm.
Purchase 109:1922

PLATE DEPICTING PUTTI AND GROTESQUERIE
Giovanni Maria
Italian, Castel Durante, first quarter 16th century
Majolica, tin-glazed earthenware, Diameter: 22.8 cm.
Purchase 72:1942

PLATE DEPICTING HERMAPHRODITUS
WITH THE NYMPH SALAMACIS, 1532
Francesco Xanto Avelli
Italian, Urbino, active 1530-42
Majolica, tin-glazed earthenware, Diameter: 26.7 cm.
Purchase 120:1951

BATTLE OF NAKED MEN, 1517
Domenico Campagnola
Italian, Padua, 1500-1581
Engraving, 22.1 x 23.0 cm.
Purchase 103:1932

PLATE
Italian, Deruta, 1st third 16th century
Majolica, tin-glazed earthenware, Diameter: 43.2 cm.
Purchase 119:1951

CHARITY
French, 16th century
Marble, Height: 68.6 cm.
Purchase 64:1928

ST. CATHERINE OF ALEXANDRIA
Antonello Gagini
Italian, Sicily, 1478-1536
Marble, Height: 167.7 cm.
Purchase 37:1936

PORTRAIT OF A MAN, ca. 1540
North Italian
Oil on panel, 80.0 x 60.0 cm.
Purchase 30:1922

MARS AND VENUS
CAUGHT IN VULCAN'S NET
Guglielmo della Porta
Italian, Rome, ca. 1516-1577
Bronze, Diameter: 14.5 cm.
Purchase 76:1945

THE CRUCIFIXION
Guglielmo della Porta
Italian, Rome, ca. 1516-1577
Bronze, 24.8 x 16.8 cm.
Purchase 43:1924

SEATED NUDE
Italo-Flemish Master, second half 16th century
Bronze, Height: 13.6 cm.
Purchase 285:1951

AN ARCHER
Italian, Venice, ca. 1600
Pen, brown ink, black chalk, 19.0 x 13.5 cm.
Purchase 1128:1940

THE BIRD CATCHER
After Giovanni da Bologna
Italian, Florence, 1524-1608
Gilt bronze, Height: 30.6 cm.
Purchase 284:1951

THE DEATH OF PROCRIS
Joachim Antonisz Wtewael
Dutch, ca. 1566-1638
Oil on canvas, 129.9 x 98.5 cm.
Purchase 198:1957

RECLINING PAN
Giovanni Angelo Montorsoli
Italian, Florence, ca. 1507-1563
Marble, Height: 64.0 cm.
Purchase 138:1947

PORTRAIT OF A MEMBER OF THE MEDICI FAMILY, Attributed to Michele Tosini, Italian, Florence, 1503-1577
Oil on panel, 102.1 x 82.5 cm., Purchase 415:1943

CHRIST SHOWN TO THE PEOPLE
Tiziano Vecellio, called Titian
Italian, Venice, ca. 1490-1576
Oil on canvas, 109.2 x 92.7 cm.
Purchase 10:1936

THE FINDING OF MOSES
Domenico Tintoretto
Italian, Venice, 1560-1635
Oil on canvas, 76.2 x 172.7 cm.
Purchase 59:1928

TRIUMPH OF VENUS
Interior of a tazza, 1546
Pierre Reymond
French, Limoges, 1513-after 1584
Monochrome enamel on copper, Diameter: 19.3 cm.
Purchase 217:1923

ALEXANDER ORDERING THE ILIAD OF HOMER TO BE PLACED IN SAFETY
THE PRIESTS OF AMMON BEFORE ALEXANDER
Jean III Pénicaud
French, Limoges, ca. 1540-after 1606
Monochrome enamel with gilt on copper, 19.7 x 22.9 cm.
Purchase 220, 221:1923

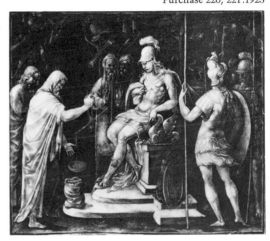

THE ENTOMBMENT
Pierre Reymond
French, Limoges, 1513-after 1584
Enamel on copper, 27.7 x 24.2 cm.
Purchase 219:1923

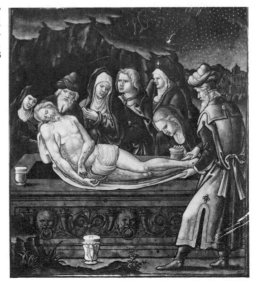

THE DEPOSITION
Pierre Reymond
French, Limoges, 1513-after 1584
Enamel on copper, 27.7 x 24.2 cm.
Purchase 218:1923

TABLE
French, 2nd half 16th century
Walnut, Height: 81.0 cm.
Purchase 88:1949

CABINET
French, 2nd half 16th century
Walnut, Height: 222.8 cm.
Purchase 44:1918

"CAQUETOIRE" CHAIR
French, 2nd half 16th century
Walnut, Height: 114.0 cm.
Purchase 166:1925

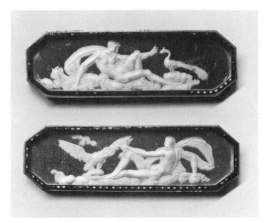

JUNO AND JUPITER
Workshop of the Saracchi
Italian, Milan, late 16th century
Rock crystal backed with mirrors
Each: 13.8 x 4.2 cm.
Purchase 154, 155:1924

BELLOWS NOZZLE
Workshop of Niccolò Roccatagliata
Italian, Venice, active 1544-1636
Bronze, Height: 26.2 cm.
Purchase 29:1925

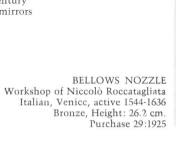

TAZZA
Italian, Milan, late 16th century
Rock crystal, gold and enamel, Height: 17.2 cm.
Purchase 53:1927

TAZZA
Italian, Venice, 2nd half 16th century
Blown glass, enameled and gilded, Diameter: 30.5 cm.
Purchase 20:1933

DOOR KNOCKER
French, 2nd half 16th century
Iron, Height: 36.4 cm.
Purchase 140:1921

Opposite, detail from:
CHRIST SHOWN TO THE PEOPLE
Jan Mostaert   207:1946
(see page 85)

CASKET
Italian, Venice, ca. 1600
Rock crystal, silver gilt and lacquered wood, Height: 47.6 cm.
Purchase: Friends Fund   346:1958

THE TREE MAN
After Hieronymous Bosch
Dutch, ca. 1450-1516
Etching, 32.0 x 25.0 cm.
Purchase: The Sidney and Sadie Cohen Print Fund   33:1971

THE OUTLINE CRUCIFIXION
Albrecht Dürer
German, 1471-1528
Engraving, 31.4 x 22.4 cm.
Purchase 138:1916

STAIRCASE
French, Morlaix, ca. 1500
Oak, Height newel post: 1330 cm.
Purchase 26:1931

CHRIST DRIVING THE MONEY CHANGERS FROM THE TEMPLE
Flemish, Brussels, ca. 1500
Wool and silk tapestry weave, 97.8 x 179.7 cm.
Purchase 185:1926

Opposite
THE PROPHECY OF NATHAN
Flemish, Brussels, early 16th century
Wool tapestry weave, 330.2 x 652.8 cm.
Gift of Leicester B. Faust and Audrey
Faust Wallace   53:1937

MILLEFLEURS TAPESTRY
French or Flemish, early 16th century
Wool tapestry weave, 312.4 x 251.5 cm.
Purchase 104:1928

THE ADORATION OF THE CHRIST CHILD
Flemish, Brussels, 1st quarter 16th century
Wool, silk, tapestry weave, 305.0 x 306.5 cm.
Purchase 287:1951

THE DESCENT FROM THE CROSS
Flemish, Brussels, ca. 1515-1520
Wool, silk, gilt, tapestry weave, 312.4 x 288.5 cm.
Purchase 286:1951

THE HOLY FAMILY
Central panel of a portable altar
Jan Gossaert, called Mabuse
Flemish, 1478-1533/36
Oil on panel, 24.5 x 21.3 cm.
Purchase 94:1947

MARY SALOME, ZEBEDEE AND THEIR SONS,
JAMES THE GREAT AND JOHN THE EVANGELIST
Hans Suess, called von Kulmbach, German, ca. 1476-1522
Oil on panel, 58.1 x 33.2 cm.
Purchase 175:1951

THE JUDGMENT OF PARIS
Lucas Cranach the Elder, German, 1472-1553
Oil and tempera on panel, 50.8 x 36.4 cm.
Purchase 28:1932

CHRIST SHOWN TO THE PEOPLE
Jan Mostaert
Dutch, ca. 1473-1555/6
Oil on panel, 55.6 x 45.8 cm.
Purchase 207:1946

ST. MARY MAGDALENE, 1519
Jacob Cornelisz
Dutch, ca. 1470 - ca. 1533
Oil on panel, 48.6 x 40.0 cm.
Gift of Edward Mallinckrodt   138:1922

THE MARRIAGE OF THE VIRGIN
The Master of 1518
Flemish, Antwerp, active ca. 1515-1530
Oil on panel, 62.8 x 69.2 cm.
Purchase 29:1929

A CANON, Johann Rieper of Brixen?
Marx Reichlich
Austrian, active 1st quarter 16th century
Oil on panel, 40.7 x 30.5 cm.
Purchase 10:1915

Opposite
LADY GULDEFORD, 1527
Hans Holbein the Younger, German, 1497/8-1543
Oil on panel, 87.0 x 70.5 cm.
Purchase 1:1943

PORTRAIT OF A MAN WITH GOLD COINS, 1522
Jean Clouet, French, ca. 1505-1540/41
Oil on panel, 42.6 x 32.4 cm.
Purchase 32:1925

ANNO·M·D·XXVII·ÆTATIS·SVÆ·XXXII.

THE CRUCIFIXION
South German, mid-16th century
Kelheim limestone with bronze tone
23.5 x 22.8 cm.
Purchase 126:1924

THE WINE PRESS OF THE WRATH OF GOD, 1561
Jean Duvet, French, 1485-after 1561
Engraving, 30.5 x 22.1 cm.
Purchase 16:1933

DON JUAN OF AUSTRIA?
Adrian Thomas Key
Flemish, ca. 1544-after 1589
Oil on panel, 44.5 x 34.3 cm.
Purchase 252:1915

PORTRAIT OF A WOMAN
Barthel Bruyn the Younger
German, ca. 1530-1610
Oil on panel, 57.2 x 43.2 cm.
Purchase 9:1915

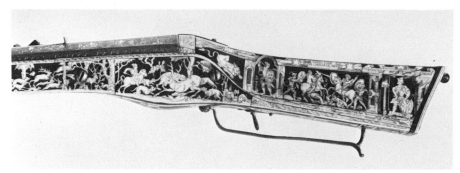

WHEELLOCK GUN, detail of stock
German, ca. 1550
Wood with staghorn inlay, Length: 120.7 cm.
Purchase 74:1939

COVERED CUP
German, 16th century
Jasper, gold and enamel, Height: 20.3 cm.
Purchase 19:1928

CABINET
Dutch or German, ca. 1550-1560
Oak with rosewood and walnut inlay
Height: 161.9 cm.
Purchase 141:1929

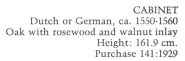

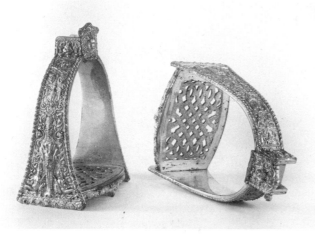

PAIR OF STIRRUPS, 1555
Attributed to Jörg Sigman
German, Augsburg, ca. 1527-1601
Gilt bronze, Height: 16.5 cm.
Purchase 54:1926

HORSE OR MULE MUZZLE
German, 2nd half 16th century
Steel, Length: 22.8 cm.
Purchase 59:1939

HELMET, mid-16th century
German, made for Eastern Europe
Steel, Height: 27.9 cm.
Purchase 71:1942

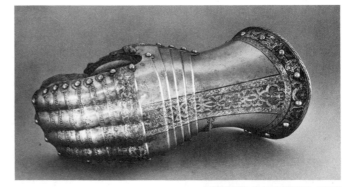

MITTEN GAUNTLET, 1563?
Attributed to Anton Peffenhauser
German, Augsburg, ca. 1525-1603
Etched, gilded and blackened steel
Length: 17.0 cm.
Purchase 80:1939

PYX
Arms of Pedro Manuel del Belmonte
Archbishop of Santiago de Compostella
Spanish, Leon, 1540-1549
Silver, Height: 22.2 cm.
Purchase 35:1921

PROCESSIONAL CROSS
Spanish, mid-16th century
Silver, Height: 97.8 cm.
Purchase 98:1957

SPHERICAL CLOCK, 1554
Jacques de la Garde
French, Blois, mid-16th century
Gilded bronze, Diameter: 12.1 cm.
Purchase 102:1926

FRAGMENT OF AN ALTAR CLOTH
Polish, ca. 1580
Embroidered linen, Length: 28.4 cm.
Purchase 52:1949

FOREST LANDSCAPE
Roelant Savery, Flemish, 1576-1639
Oil on panel, 30.2 x 44.0 cm.
Purchase 170:1953

FLOWERS, 1622
Balthasar van der Ast
Dutch, 1593/4-1657
Oil on copper, 33.5 x 22.2 cm.
Purchase 172:1955

Opposite
TERRESTRIAL GLOBE, 1613
Jodocus Hondius, Jodocus Hondius, Jr.,
Adrianus Veen, Dutch, worked early 17th Century
Engraving, tinted paper, wood core,
Walnut stand, Height: 72.4 cm.
Purchase: Ellis Wainwright Fund   113:1946

STILL LIFE, 1619
Lodewijck Susi
Flemish, mentioned 1616-1620
Oil on panel, 34.9 x 46.5 cm.
Purchase 50:1949

A SMILING GIRL, 1625
Gerrit van Honthorst, Dutch, 1590-1656
Oil on canvas, 81.3 x 64.3 cm.
Purchase: Friends Fund   63:1954

SUFFER THE CHILDREN TO COME UNTO ME
Jacob Jordaens, Flemish, 1593-1678
Oil on canvas, 104.2 x 169.8 cm.
Purchase 7:1956

STILL LIFE, 1643
Pieter Claesz
Dutch, 1597/8-1661
Oil on panel, 62.2 x 48.3 cm.
Purchase 141:1922

MARQUIS AMBROGIO SPINOLA
Peter Paul Rubens and Assistants, Flemish, 1577-1640
Oil on canvas, 118.1 x 85.4 cm.
Purchase 33:1934

PORTRAIT OF A WOMAN, ca. 1625-30
Attributed to Pieter Claesz Soutman, Dutch, ?-1657
Oil on canvas, 117.8 x 91.4 cm.
Gift of Edward Mallinckrodt   139:1922

PORTRAIT OF A LADY, ca. 1650-55, Frans Hals, Dutch, 1581/5-1666, Oil on canvas, 102.5 x 88.9 cm., Purchase and Friends Fund   272:1955

WINTER LANDSCAPE
Hendrick Avercamp
Dutch, 1585 - ca. 1663
Oil on panel, 33.1 x 61.0 cm.
Purchase 46:1939

SKATING ON THE ICE NEAR DORDRECHT, 1643
Jan van Goyen, Dutch, 1596-1656
Oil on panel, 37.5 x 34.3 cm.
Purchase 223:1916

Preceding page, detail from FOREST LANDSCAPE, Roelant Savery, 170:1953, see page 93

LANDSCAPE, ca. 1640, Aelbert Cuyp, Dutch, 1620-1691, Oil on Panel, 76.9 x 107.2 cm., Purchase: Friends Fund   23:1967

INTERIOR SCENE WITH PEASANTS DANCING, 1659
Adriaen van Ostade
Dutch, 1610-1684
Oil on panel, 44.2 x 60.3 cm.
Purchase: Friends Fund   147:1966

KITCHEN INTERIOR
Willem Kalf
Dutch, 1619-1693
Oil on panel, 25.4 x 21.0 cm.
Purchase 93:1947

THE HOUSEKEEPER, 1656
Nicholaes Maes
Dutch, 1632-1693
Oil on canvas, 66.4 x 53.7 cm.
Purchase 72:1950

A YOUNG MAN, 1662, Rembrandt van Rijn, Dutch, 1606-1669, Oil on canvas, 89.9 x 70.8 cm., Purchase 90:1950

JACOB DE GRAEFF
Gerard Ter Borch
Dutch, 1617-1681
Oil on panel, 54.6 x 35.6 cm.
Purchase 139:1916

THE STREET MUSICIANS, 1665
Jacob Ochtervelt
Dutch, 1634/5-by 1710
Oil on canvas, 68.6 x 57.2 cm.
Gift of Mrs. Eugene A. Perry   162:1928

KING DAVID, THE PROPHET GAD
AND THE ANGEL OF DEATH
Abraham van Diepenbeeck
Flemish, 1596-1675
Pen, brown ink, white heightening
over black chalk, 34.0 x 21.1 cm.
Purchase: Funds given by Mr. and Mrs.
Lansing W. Thoms   206:1966

KNEELING WOMAN, 1620
Giovanni Mannozzi, called da San Giovanni
Italian, Florence, 1592-1636
Black chalk, 41.1 x 23.8 cm.
Purchase 138:1966

THE TEMPTATION OF ST. ANTHONY
Giovanni Francesco Barbieri, called Guercino
Italian, Bologna, 1591-1666
Red chalk, 35.9 x 32.9 cm.
Purchase: Funds given by Oliver M. Langenberg
124:1966

Below left

ST. LAWRENCE DISTRIBUTING THE RICHES OF THE CHURCH
Bernardo Strozzi, Italian, Genoa, 1581-1644
Oil on canvas, 121.9 x 162.5 cm., Purchase 37:1944

A MUSICAL PARTY, ca. 1625-30, Nicolas Tournier, French, 1590-after 1657, Oil on canvas, 120.5 x 165.4 cm. Purchase 90:1942

ST. JOHN THE BAPTIST PREACHING
IN THE WILDERNESS, ca. 1660
Salvator Rosa
Italian, Naples, 1615-1673
Oil on canvas, 200.7 x 121.9 cm.
Purchase: Friends Fund   72:1970

ST. PAUL, ca. 1605-10
Domenikos Theotocopoulos, called El Greco
Spanish, 1541-1614
Oil on canvas, 69.9 x 55.9 cm.
Purchase 1:1936

ABRAHAM AND THE THREE ANGELS, ca. 1650
Giovanni Andrea de'Ferrari
Italian, Genoa, 1598-1669
Oil on canvas, 205.7 x 238.7 cm.
Purchase 45:1939

CHRIST HEALING THE BLIND, 1682
Nicolas Colombel, French, 1644-1717
Oil on canvas, 118.5 x 87.8 cm.
Gift of Mrs. Bradford Shinkle,
Mrs. J. Russell Forgan and Andrew W. Johnson
12:1957

CHRIST DRIVING THE MONEY CHANGERS FROM
THE TEMPLE, 1682
Nicolas Colombel, French, 1644-1717
Oil on canvas, 118.5 x 87.7 cm.
Gift of Mrs. Bradford Shinkle,
Mrs. J. Russell Forgan and Andrew W. Johnson 11:1957

MADONNA AND CHILD
Giuseppe Mazza
Bologna, 1653-1741
Painted terra-cotta, Diameter: 15.6 cm.
Purchase and Gift of Mrs. Robert Corley   138:1965

THE CASTAWAYS
Alessandro Magnasco
Genoa, 1667-1749
Oil on canvas, 112.5 x 172.7 cm.
Purchase 1136:1940

JUDITH WITH
THE HEAD OF HOLOFERNES, 1704
Luca Giordano, Naples, 1632-1705
Oil on canvas, 76.4 x 102.2 cm.
Purchase 60:1965

THE DISCOVERY OF
THE BODY OF HOLOFERNES, 1704
Luca Giordano, Naples, 1632-1705
Oil on canvas, 76.4 x 102.2 cm.
Purchase 61:1965

HOLY WATER FONT
Giuseppe Piamontini
Florence, 1664-1742
Gilt bronze, Height: 71.4 cm.
Purchase: Friends Fund 169:1966

THE MARRIAGE OF HERCULES AND HEBE, 1729
Carlo Innocenzo Carlone, Lombardy, 1686-1775
Pen, ink and gray washes over black chalk
37.0 x 50.0 cm.
Purchase and Bequest of Oliver F. Peters 107:1970

SCULPTURE AND ARCHITECTURE
Francesco Bertos, Venice, active 1693-1733
Bronze, Height of tallest: 33.7 cm.
Purchase 298:1955 .2, .1

HERCULES
Massimiliano Soldani
Florence, 1658-1740
Bronze, Height: 30.5 cm.
Purchase 11:1922

INTERIOR OF ST. PETER'S, ROME, 1731, Giovanni Paolo Panini, Rome, 1691-1765, Oil on canvas, 145.2 x 227.5 cm., Purchase 7:1946

THE EMPEROR CONSTANTINE
PRESENTED TO THE HOLY TRINITY
BY HIS MOTHER, ST. HELENA, 1744
Corrado Giaquinto, Naples, 1699-1765
Oil on canvas, 346.8 x 143.5 cm.
Purchase 31:1963

THE CONQUEST OF ACRI
Giovanni Antonio Guardi
Venice, 1698-1760
Pen, brown wash over black chalk
52.8 x 77.6 cm.
Purchase 40:1954

THE EXPULSION OF ADAM AND EVE, 1758
Filippo Scandellari, Bologna, 1717-1801
Painted terra-cotta, 66.0 x 44.5 cm.
Purchase 1:1965

MASKED PARTY IN A COURTYARD, 1755
Pietro Longhi, Venice, 1707-1785
Oil on canvas, 61.0 x 50.8 cm.
Purchase 32:1939

CHRIST HEALING THE PARALYTIC
Giovanni Domenico Tiepolo, Venice, 1727-1804
Pen, brown ink over black chalk, 48.6 x 38.1 cm.
Purchase 113:1954

CAPRICCIO: AN ISLAND IN THE LAGOON WITH A PAVILION AND A CHURCH
Antonio Canal, called Canaletto, Venice, 1697-1768
Oil on canvas, 51.2 x 68.6 cm.
Purchase: Friends Fund   12:1967

SIX FIGURES
Giovanni Battista Piranesi
Rome, 1720-1778
Red and red-brown chalk, 18.4 x 15.2 cm.
Purchase 143:1953

THE CRUCIFIXION
Giovanni Domenico Tiepolo
Venice, 1727-1804
Oil on canvas, 79.4 x 88.3 cm.
Purchase 10:1940

CARDINAL JEAN DE ROCHECHOUART, 1762, Pompeo Girolamo Batoni, Rome, 1708-1787
Oil on canvas, 136.2 x 98.4 cm., Purchase: Friends Fund 135:1972

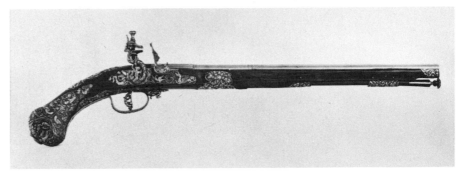

FLINTLOCK PISTOL, ca. 1680, Lazaro Lazarino, Italian, Brescia
Walnut with steel mounts, Length: 55.7 cm., Purchase 78:1939

SCALES
Luis Diaz
Spanish, Madrid, 17th century
Steel, Height: 68.6 cm.
Purchase 113:1922

WHEELLOCK RIFLE, 1623
Claude Thomas, French, Epinal, active early 17th century
Pearwood and steel, Length: 120.5 cm.
Purchase 70:1939

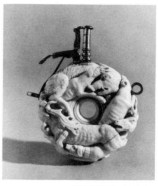

POWDER TESTER, Picino Frusca, Italian, Brescia, 1640-1704
Rosewood, gilt bronze and steel, Length: 23.3 cm.
Purchase 24:1925

POWDER FLASK
German, 17th century
Ivory with brass mounts
Height: 11.6 cm.
Purchase 121:1924

BOX
Attributed to the Bagard
French, Nancy, late 17th century
Wood, Height: 11.1 cm.
Purchase 74:1924

ST. SEBASTIAN
German, 17th century
Pearwood and boxwood, Height: 39.4 cm.
Purchase 487:1955

BOWL, 1687
German, probably Frankfurt
Tin-glazed earthenware
Diameter: 22.2 cm.
Gift of
Mrs. Norman Frederick Mack
538:1957

JAR, ca. 1700
Dutch, possibly Amsterdam
Tin-glazed, enameled earthenware
Height: 36.5 cm.
Purchase 491:1955

LATTACINO WINE GLASS
Italian, Venice, ca. 1600
Glass, Height: 17.5 cm.
Gift of Mrs. Hugo Koehler   93:1945

WINE GLASS
German, Nuremberg, ca. 1650-1700
Enameled glass, Height: 12.0 cm.
Gift of Mrs. Hugo Koehler   101:1945

BEAKER
German, probably Nuremberg, 17th century
Blown glass, wheel-engraved, Height: 13.7 cm.
Purchase 10:1926

ESTHER AND AHASUERUS, English, 2nd half 17th century
Embroidered linen, 32.3 x 44.5 cm., Gift of Mrs. William A. McDonnell   6:1972

KING SOLOMON AND THE QUEEN OF SHEBA
English, 2nd half 17th century
Embroidered silk, satin weave, 29.9 x 41.3 cm.
Gift of Mrs. William A. McDonnell 5:1972

JACOB'S DREAM
English, early 18th century
Embroidered silk, satin weave, 47.0 x 43.5 cm.
Gift of Mrs. William A. McDonnell 9:1972

PORRINGER AND COVER, ca. 1678
T.K., English, London, active 1663-94
Silver, Height: 19.1 cm.
Purchase 56:1924

SUGAR CASTER, 1702
Joseph Ward, English, active 1697-1717
Britannia silver, Height: 17.9 cm.
Purchase 822:1940

MONTEITH, 1709
Edmund Pearce, English, London
Silver, Height: 22.2 cm.
Purchase 820:1940

HOPE
German, early 18th century
Bronze, Height: 48.6 cm.
Purchase 224:1945

LENGTH OF FABRIC
Probably French, early 18th century
Silk damask, brocaded, Length: 203.3 cm.
Purchase 23:1931

PRUDENCE
German, early 18th century
Bronze, Height: 51.0 cm.
Purchase 223:1945

PART TEA AND COFFEE SERVICE, ca. 1733, Arms of the 9th Duke of Norfolk, German, Meissen, in the manner Of Johann G. Höroldt, Porcelain, overglaze enamels and gilt, Height of coffee pot: 17.9 cm., Purchase 38-54:1945

VASES FROM THE "SWAN" SERVICE, ca. 1737-41, Johann Joachim Kändler, 1706-1775, Johann Friederich Eberlein, 1696-1749 German, Meissen, Gilded porcelain, Height: 58.2 cm., Purchase 36, 37:1945

WINE GLASS
German, probably Berlin, ca. 1740
Wheel-engraved glass, Height: 18.1 cm.
Gift of Mrs. Hugo Koehler 90:1945

AUGUSTUS III, ELECTOR OF SAXONY AND KING OF POLAND
Johann Joachim Kändler, 1706-1775
German, Meissen, ca. 1744
Porcelain, Height: 43.4 cm.
Purchase 256:1951

COVERED CUP "THE ASHBROOK CUP," 1749
Frederick Kandler, English, London
Silver, Height: 42.9 cm.
Gift of Morton J. May 252:1952

CUP, 1733/34
Claude Alexis Moulienau, French, Paris
Silver, Height: 9.5 cm.
Purchase 102:1939

COVERED DISH, 1740-42
Alexis Loir III, French, Paris, 1712-1785
Silver, Height: 12.5 cm.
Purchase 101:1939

EWER AND BASIN, 1740
Jean Fauche, French
Silver, Height of ewer: 23.8 cm.
Purchase 96, 97:1939

CUP, French, last quarter 18th century
Rock crystal, gilt bronze
Height: 12.1 cm.
Purchase 75:1924

BOWL WITH COVER AND STAND, ca. 1753
Decorated by Philippe Xhrouet, active 1750-75
French, Vincennes
Porcelain, overglaze enamel, gilded, Height: 14.3 cm.
Purchase 7:1945

SCONCES
French, last quarter 18th century
Gilt bronze, Height: 81.0 cm.
Purchase 110, 111:1917

SECRETARY
French, ca. 1790-1800
Inlaid, painted, gilded mahogany, ormolu
Height: 125.8 cm.
Purchase 365:1923

CORNER CABINET, 1785
Jean Henri Riesener, French, 1734-1806
Mahogany, marble, ormolu mounts, Height: 91.0 cm.
Purchase 117:1945

THE SILVER GOBLET, ca. 1730
Jean-Baptiste Siméon Chardin, 1699-1779
Oil on canvas, 42.9 x 48.3 cm.
Purchase 55:1934

THE WASHERWOMEN
Jean-Honoré Fragonard, 1732-1806
Oil on canvas, 61.6 x 73.1 cm.
Purchase 76:1937

MADAME DE LA MARTELLIERE, Nicolas de Largillière, 1656-1746, Oil on canvas, 159.8 x 127.3 cm., Purchase 3:1943

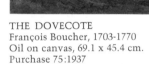

THE DOVECOTE
François Boucher, 1703-1770
Oil on canvas, 69.1 x 45.4 cm.
Purchase 75:1937

THE BAPTISM OF CHRIST
François Boucher, 1703-1770
Pen, brown ink over black chalk
25.6 x 19.8 cm.
Purchase 180:1955

FETE GALANTE
Jean-Baptiste Joseph Pater, 1695-1736
Oil on canvas, 54.6 x 65.7 cm.
Purchase: Friends Fund 13:1967

TWO COURTESANS, 1799
Henry Fuseli, Swiss, 1741-1825
Black and brown chalk, 27.7 x 19.0 cm.
Purchase 144:1953

AUGUSTIN AND HIS FAMILY, 1800
Jean-Baptiste-Jacques Augustin, 1759-1832
Black and white chalk, 23.3 x 33.2 cm.
Purchase: Funds given by
Mr. and Mrs. G. Gordon Hertslet   56:1967

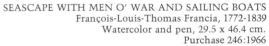

MADAME DU BARRY, ca. 1771
Jean-Baptiste Lemoyne II, 1704-1778
Terra-cotta, Height: 35.6 cm.
Purchase: Friends Fund 1:1967

BENJAMIN FRANKLIN, 1778
Jean-Antoine Houdon, 1741-1828
Plaster, Height: 44.5 cm.
Purchase 32:1935

SEASCAPE WITH MEN O' WAR AND SAILING BOATS
François-Louis-Thomas Francia, 1772-1839
Watercolor and pen, 29.5 x 46.4 cm.
Purchase 246:1966

FANTASY ON TIVOLI, 1789, Hubert Robert, 1733-1808, Oil on canvas, 241.1 x 193.4 cm., Gift of Mrs. Frederic W. Allen   524:1955

Preceding page, detail from
Thomas Gainsborough
VIEW IN SUFFOLK   168:1928
See page 135

LORDS JOHN AND BERNARD STUART
After Sir Anthony van Dyck
Thomas Gainsborough, 1727-1788
Oil on canvas, 235.0 x 146.1 cm.
Gift of Mrs. Jackson Johnson   15:1943

PORTRAIT OF A MAN
Francis Hayman, 1708-1776
Oil on canvas, 63.5 x 76.5 cm.
Purchase 73:1945

VIEW IN SUFFOLK
Thomas Gainsborough, 1727-1788
Oil on canvas, 94.0 x 125.7 cm.
Bequest of Mrs. Cora Liggett Fowler
168:1928

JOHN JULIUS ANGERSTEIN, 1765
Sir Joshua Reynolds, 1723-1792
Oil on canvas, 91.5 x 71.1 cm.
Purchase 107:1922

PORTRAIT OF A LADY
George Romney, 1734-1802
Oil on canvas, 76.2 x 63.5 cm.
Bequest of Edward Mallinckrodt, Sr.   28:1974

MRS. ROBERT GWILLYM, 1766
Joseph Wright of Derby, 1734-1797
Oil on canvas, 127.0 x 101.6 cm.
Purchase: Funds given by
Miss Martha I. Love   72:1965

ROBERT GWILLYM, 1766
Joseph Wright of Derby, 1734-1797
Oil on canvas, 127.0 x 101.6 cm.
Purchase: Funds given by
Miss Martha I. Love   71:1965

PORTRAIT OF A MAN, 1792
Thomas Robinson, Irish, ca. 1770-1810
Oil on canvas, 74.9 x 62.3 cm.
Purchase 42:1918

Opposite
HENRY ADDINGTON,
FIRST VISCOUNT SIDMOUTH, ca. 1797/8
John Singleton Copley
Anglo-American, 1738-1815
Oil on canvas, 237.6 x 162.6 cm.
Purchase 26:1929

ANNE PRINGLE, ca. 1813
Henry Raeburn, Scot, 1756-1823
Oil on canvas, 76.7 x 63.5 cm.
Gift of Sydney M. Shoenberg   288:1948

VISCOUNTESS BULKELEY AS HEBE, 1776
George Romney, 1734-1802
Pen, brown ink and wash over pencil
46.4 x 27.1 cm.
Purchase 27:1942

PORTRAIT OF A WOMAN
George Engleheart, 1750-1829
Gouache on ivory, Height: 5.6 cm.
Purchase 107:1930

PORTRAIT OF A MAN
Richard Cosway, 1742-1821
Gouache on ivory, Height: 7.6 cm.
Purchase 160:1924

PORTRAIT OF A WOMAN, 1760
Nathaniel Hone, Irish, 1718-1784
Oil on porcelain, Height: 3.3 cm.
Gift of Winslow Ames   98:1952

BANDITTI REGALING, 1772 (?)
John Hamilton Mortimer, 1741-1779
Pen and black ink, 39.0 x 43.7 cm.
Purchase: Funds given by
Mr. and Mrs. Christian B. Peper   82:1969

DISH, ca. 1715
John III Simpson, North Staffordshire, 1685-1774
Lead-glazed, slip decorated earthenware
Width: 33.7 cm.
Purchase: Funds given by The Measuregraph Company   19:1971

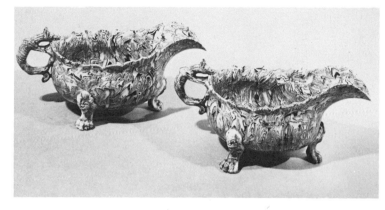

PAIR OF SAUCE BOATS, ca. 1750
Attributed to Thomas Whieldon, 1719-1795
Staffordshire
Lead-glazed agate earthenware, Height: 8.7 cm.
Purchase 125:1966

PAIR OF SAUCE BOATS, ca. 1755-65
Attributed to
William Reid and Company, Liverpool
Overglaze enameled porcelain
Length: 20.3 cm.
Purchase: Funds given by
Various donors   145:1972

PAIR OF FLOWER HOLDERS, ca. 1750-60
Staffordshire
Salt-glazed stoneware, Height: 7.6 cm.
Purchase: Decorative Arts Society Fund   5:1971

CAULIFLOWER TEAPOT, ca. 1765-70
Wedgwood-Greatbatch factory, Staffordshire
Lead-glazed earthenware, Height: 13.3 cm.
Gift of Mr. and Mrs. Roland Jester   114:1962

RETICULATED BOWL, ca. 1741-60
Attributed to Longton Hall, Staffordshire
Blue salt-glazed stoneware, Height: 8.2 cm.
Purchase: Funds given by various donors   165:1966

PINEAPPLE BOWL, ca. 1754-59
Whieldon-Wedgwood factory, Staffordshire
Lead-glazed earthenware, Height: 7.0 cm.
Gift of Mr. and Mrs. Roland Jester   117:1962

COFFEE POT, 1736
Joseph Smith, London, active mid-18th century
Silver, Height: 21.4 cm.
Gift of Mrs. Arthur Drefs 219:1957

TEA CASKET, ca. 1770
South Staffordshire, probably Bilston
Enameled copper, gilt copper mounts
Height: 13.3 cm.
Purchase: Decorative Arts Society Fund
73:1973

PAIR OF COVERED HEXAGONAL JARS
Worcester, ca. 1765-70
Porcelain, underglaze blue
Overglaze enamels and gilt, Height: 29.2 cm.
Purchase and Decorative Arts Society Fund
78:1973

SIDE CHAIR, ca. 1720
Walnut, Height: 99.4 cm.
Purchase 828:1940

SOFA, ca. 1740
Mahogany, Height: 114.3 cm.
Gift of Joseph Pulitzer   45:1929

COVERLET, ca. 1780-1800
Chinese, made for the Western market
Embroidered silk, satin weave, 276.5 x 226.5 cm.
Gift of Mr. and Mrs. Richard Kent 51:1960

SECRETARY BOOKCASE
Last quarter 18th century
Mahogany, Height: 269.3 cm.
Purchase 118:1917

SIDE TABLE
Irish, third quarter 18th century
Mahogany, Height: 83.2 cm.
Purchase 827:1940

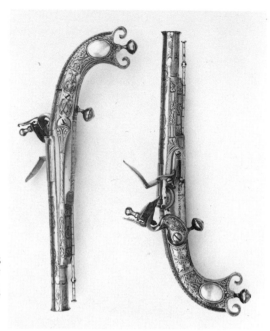

REPEATING FLINTLOCK PISTOL
Paris of Derby, English, active 1775-85
Walnut, silver wire, gilded and blued steel, Length: 29.3 cm.
Purchase 43:1939

PAIR OF FLINTLOCK PISTOLS
John Murdoch, Scot, active second half 18th century
Engraved steel, silver inlay, Length: 29.3 cm.
Purchase 4, 5:1943

SET OF PISTOLS AND ACCESSORIES, 1799
Iacinto Xavier, Portuguese, Lisbon, active late 18th century
Walnut, silver inlay, gilded and blued steel, Purchase 185:1942

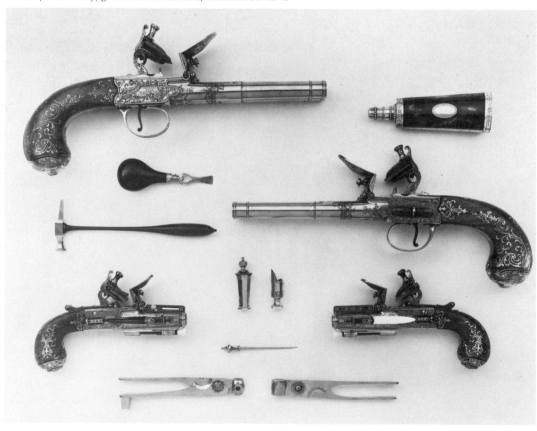

HOT WATER JUG, 1812-13
Paul Storr, English, London, 1771-1844
Silver, Height: 23.2 cm.
Purchase 6:1935

PAIR OF CANDELABRA
French, ca. 1804-15
Gilt bronze, Height: 86.4 cm.
Gift of Virgil A. Lewis   53:1970

COVERED TUREEN AND TRAY, 1797-98
Henri Auguste, French, Paris, 1759-1816
Silver, Height: 29.4 cm.
Gift of James H. Hyde   414:1952

TUMBLER
Russian, Bakmetev Factory, ca. 1810-20
Double-walled glass with montage
Height: 11.5 cm.
Gift of Mrs. Hugo Koehler   109:1945

PAIR OF WINE COASTERS, 1806
Benjamin Smith and Digby Scott
English, London
Gilded silver, Height: 8.1 cm.
Purchase 1082:1920

Opposite
MERCURY AND MARS
French, ca. 1800-10
Appliquéd and embroidered silk
251.5 x 88.9 cm.
Purchase 364, 363:1923

TABLE CENTERPIECE, ca. 1810-20
Pierre Philippe Thomire
French, Paris, 1751-1843
Gilded bronze, Height: 76.5 cm.
Gift of Alphonse Raes   106:1954

JOHN RUSSELL, SIXTH DUKE OF BEDFORD, 1815
Jean-Auguste-Dominique Ingres
French, 1780-1867
Pencil, 38.8 x 29.2 cm.
Purchase 354:1952

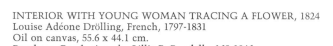

VALLEY IN THE AUVERGNE MOUNTAINS, 1830
Théodore Rousseau, French, 1812-1867
Oil on paper, 21.7 x 31.1 cm.
Purchase: Friends Fund   170:1966

Opposite, from top left
All gouache on ivory, shown actual size

JOSEPH B. LITTLEJOHN, 1800, Louis Marie Sicardi, French, 1746-1825
Gift of Mrs. John L. Swasey   123:1971

PORTRAIT OF A MAN, Louis Marie Sicardi, French, 1746-1825
M. FARDIEU, Jean Baptiste Isabey, French, 1767-1855
PORTRAIT OF A MAN, Moritz Michael Daffinger, Austrian, 1790-1849
Gift of Mrs. Frank Spiekerman   28:1933.36,.77,.15

INTERIOR WITH YOUNG WOMAN TRACING A FLOWER, 1824
Louise Adéone Drölling, French, 1797-1831
Oil on canvas, 55.6 x 44.1 cm.
Purchase: Funds given by Lillie B. Randell   160:1946

THE STONE BREAKER, 1830
Nicolas-Toussaint Charlet
French, 1792-1845
Lithograph, 33.2 x 27.0 cm.
Purchase: Sidney and Sadie Cohen
Print Fund   203:1966

NUDE FIGURE, 1848
William Mulready, Irish, 1786-1863
Red chalk and pencil, 36.7 x 27.3 cm.
Purchase: Funds given by
Mr. and Mrs. Christian B. Peper   38:1972

THE STREET SINGER
Honoré Daumier, French, 1808-1879
Black chalk, 24.4 x 27.9 cm.
Purchase: Friends Fund   4:1957

THE KNITTING SHEPHERDESS, ca. 1856-57
Jean François Millet, French, 1814-1875
Pastel, 33.7 x 25.4 cm.
Gift of the J. Lionberger Davis Art Trust Fund
156:1953

THE GOOD SAMARITAN, 1861
Rodolphe Bresdin, French, 1825-1885
Lithograph, 56.8 x 44.8 cm.
Purchase: Friends Fund   35:1972

PORTRAIT OF A WOMAN, 1853-54
Gustave Courbet, 1819-1877
Oil on canvas, 127.0 x 100.4 cm.
Gift of Joseph Pulitzer, Jr.   271:1972

COMTESSE DE VALMONT
Jean François Millet, 1814-1875
Oil on canvas, 98.7 x 79.7 cm.
Purchase 76:1954

THE RACES, 1865
Edouard Manet, 1832-1883
Lithograph, 38.6 x 51.0 cm.
Bequest of Horace M. Swope   643:1940

THE CAPTURE OF WEISLINGEN, 1853
Eugène Delacroix, 1798-1863
Oil on canvas, 73.2 x 59.7 cm.
Purchase: Emelie Weindal
Bequest Fund   75:1954

THE TWO SISTERS, 1859,
Henri Fantin-Latour, 1836-1904,
Oil on canvas, 98.0 x 130.0 cm.
Purchase 8:1937

GIRL WITH MANDOLIN, ca. 1860-65
Jean-Baptiste-Camille Corot, 1796-1875
Oil on canvas, 51.4 x 36.8 cm.
Purchase 3:1939

THE READER, ca. 1861
Edouard Manet, 1832-1883
Oil on canvas, 97.8 x 80.0 cm.
Purchase 254:1915

BEACH SCENE, 1865
Eugène Boudin, 1824-1898
Pencil and watercolor, 11.4 x 22.9 cm.
Purchase 109:1939

THE MARTYRED ST. SEBASTIAN, 1869
Gustave Moreau, 1826-1898
Oil on panel, 32.1 x 23.7 cm.
Purchase 19:1968

THE GREYHOUNDS OF THE COMTE DE CHOISEUL, 1866
Gustave Courbet, 1819-1877
Oil on canvas, 88.9 x 116.2 cm.
Gift of Mrs. Mark C. Steinberg   168:1953

THE BEACH, ETRETAT
Jean-Baptiste-Camille Corot, 1796-1875
Oil on canvas, 35.6 x 57.2 cm.
Purchase 63:1932

THE ARTIST'S FATHER, 1869
Pierre Auguste Renoir, 1841-1919
Oil on canvas, 61.0 x 45.7 cm.
Purchase 37:1933

THE KNITTING LESSON, 1869
Jean François Millet, 1814-1875
Oil on canvas, 101.0 x 57.2 cm.
Purchase 106:1939

ST. JOHN THE BAPTIST, 1878
Auguste Rodin, 1840-1917
Bronze, Height: 201.3 cm.
Purchase 2:1946

BUST OF VICTOR HUGO, 1883
Auguste Rodin, 1840-1917
Bronze, Height: 42.9 cm.
Bequest of Edward Mallinckrodt, Sr.
50:1967

OSTEND FISHERMAN
Constantin Meunier
Belgian, 1831-1905
Bronze, Height: 80.7 cm.
Purchase 54:1914

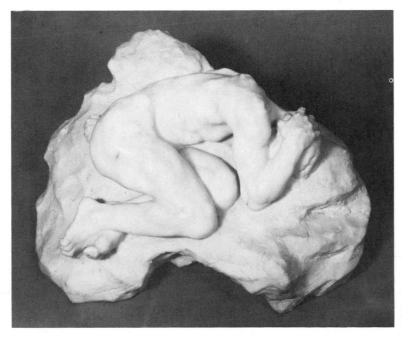

DESPAIR
Auguste Rodin, 1840-1917
Marble, Height: 34.9 cm.
Purchase 58:1921

GALLOPING HORSE, 1865-81
Edgar Degas, 1834-1917
Bronze, Height: 31.1 cm.
Purchase 187:1946

BALLET DANCERS IN THE WINGS, ca. 1895
Edgar Degas, 1834-1917
Pastel, 71.1 x 66.0 cm.
Purchase 24:1935

BALLET DANCER, 1880.
Edgar Degas, 1834-1917
Bronze, gauze and satin ribbon, Height: 97.6 cm.
Gift of Mrs. Mark C. Steinberg   135:1956

ASTERS IN A VASE, 1875
Henri Fantin Latour, 1836-1904
Oil on canvas, 57.8 x 59.1 cm.
Purchase 4:1944

THE DREAMER, 1879
Pierre Auguste Renoir, 1841-1919
Oil on canvas, 49.5 x 59.7 cm.
Purchase 5:1935

THE RIVER BANK AT SAINT-MAMMES, 1884
Alfred Sisley, 1839-1899
Oil on canvas, 50.8 x 62.2 cm.
Purchase 224:1916

THE RAILROAD BRIDGE AT ARGENTEUIL, ca. 1875-77
Claude Monet, 1840-1926
Oil on canvas, 54.3 x 72.4 cm.
Gift of Sydney M. Shoenberg, Sr.   45:1973

CHARING CROSS BRIDGE, 1903
Claude Monet, 1840-1926
Oil on canvas, 73.7 x 100.3 cm.
Purchase 22:1915

THE LOUVRE: MORNING, 1901
Camille Pissarro, 1830-1903
Oil on canvas, 73.7 x 92.7 cm.
Purchase 225:1916

LES NYMPHEAS, 1920-22, Claude Monet, 1840-1926, Oil on canvas, 200.0 x 426.2 cm., Gift of the Steinberg Charitable Fund 134:1956

COVER AND TWO PAGES FROM:
"L'ESPRIT MODERNE ET LE CATHOLICISME," 1897-98
Paul Gauguin, 1848-1903
Traced monotype, 31.8 x 19.2 cm.
Gift of Vincent Price   287:1948

MADAME ROULIN, 1888
Paul Gauguin, 1848-1903
Oil on canvas, 48.9 x 62.2 cm.
Gift of Mrs. Mark C. Steinberg
5:1959

STILL LIFE WITH APPLES, 1887
Vincent van Gogh, Dutch, 1853-1890
Oil on canvas, 46.7 x 55.2 cm.
Gift of Sydney M. Shoenberg, Sr.   43:1972

THE HUTH FACTORIES AT CLICHY, 1887
Vincent van Gogh, Dutch, 1853-1890
Oil on canvas, 53.9 x 72.9 cm.
Gift of Mrs. Mark C. Steinberg   579:1958

PORT-EN-BESSIN: THE OUTER
HARBOR (LOW TIDE), 1888
Georges Seurat, 1859-1891
Oil on canvas, 53.7 x 65.7 cm.
Purchase 4:1934

STAIRWAY AT AUVERS, 1890
Vincent van Gogh, Dutch, 1853-1890
Oil on canvas, 50.8 x 71.1 cm.
Purchase 1:1935

THE BATHERS, 1897
Paul Cézanne, 1839-1906
Lithograph, 28.7 x 35.6 cm.
Gift of Horace M. Swope   144:1940

THE ARTIST'S SISTER, ca. 1867-69
Paul Cézanne, 1839-1906
Oil on canvas, 53.3 x 36.8 cm.
Purchase 34:1934

CORNER OF LAKE ANNECY, 1897
Paul Cézanne, 1839-1906
Watercolor, 46.0 x 59.1 cm.
Purchase 52:1948

THE ART DEALERS:
THE BERNHEIM BROTHERS, 1908
Edouard Vuillard, 1868-1940
Oil on canvas, 73.2 x 66.0 cm.
Gift of Mr. and Mrs. Richard K. Weil
66:1953

THE FIRE-PLACE, 1901
Edouard Vuillard, 1868-1940
Oil on paper, 44.8 x 60.6 cm.
Gift of Mr. and Mrs. John Simon   177:1955

THE GOSSIP, 1904
Jacques Villon, French, 1875-1963
Aquatint and drypoint, 41.6 x 57.2 cm.
Purchase: Sidney and Sadie Cohen Print Fund 135:1966

Preceding page, detail from
Henri Matisse
BATHERS WITH A TURTLE   24:1964
See page 173

POSTER FOR "LE SALON DES CENT," 1896
Pierre Bonnard, French, 1867-1947
Lithograph, 61.5 x 42.0 cm.
Purchase: Sidney and Sadie Cohen Print Fund   197:1966

MOONLIGHT, 1896
Edvard Munch, Norwegian, 1863-1944
Woodcut, 40.0 x 47.0 cm.
Gift of General and Mrs. Leif J. Sverdrup   338:1952

AT THE SURESNES BALL, 1903, André Derain, French, 1880-1954, Oil on canvas, 180.0 x 144.9 cm., Purchase 172:1944

RUSSIAN BEGGAR WOMAN, 1906
Ernst Barlach, German, 1870-1938
Porcelain, Height: 24.1 cm.
Gift of Mr. and Mrs. Morton D. May   663:1958

THE MOTHER, 1901
Pablo Picasso, Spanish, 1881-1973
Oil on pulpboard, 74.9 x 51.4 cm.
Purchase 10:1939

DECORATIVE FIGURE, 1908
Henri Matisse, French, 1869-1954
Bronze, Height: 72.1 cm.
Gift of Mr. and Mrs. Richard K. Weil   173:1959

BATHERS WITH A TURTLE, 1908, Henri Matisse, French, 1869-1954
Oil on canvas, 179.1 x 220.3 cm., Gift of Mr. and Mrs. Joseph Pulitzer, Jr.   24:1964

TEMPTATION, 1912
Marc Chagall, Russian, born 1887
Oil on canvas, 160.5 x 114.0 cm.
Gift of Morton D. May   74:1954

THE TRANSFORMED DREAM, 1913
Giorgio de Chirico, Italian, born 1888
Oil on canvas, 62.9 x 152.1 cm.
Anonymous Gift   313:1951

STANDING NUDE, 1913
Ernst Ludwig Kirchner, German, 1880-1938
Wood, Height: 66.0 cm.
Gift of Mr. and Mrs. Morton D. May   402:1955

THE IMP, 1914
Henry Gaudier-Brzeska, French, 1891-1915
Charcoal on tan paper, 24.1 x 15.6 cm.
Purchase 15:1942

TWO NUDES
Ernst Ludwig Kirchner, German, 1880-1938
Pastel and charcoal, 66.0 x 49.7 cm.
Gift of Morton D. May   357:1955

LANDSCAPE WITH ANIMALS, 1913
Franz Marc, German, 1880-1916
Gouache and watercolor, 45.1 x 36.8 cm.
Gift of Morton D. May   374:1955

FOX, 1911
Georges Braque, French, 1882-1963
Etching, 54.6 x 38.1 cm.
Purchase: Sidney and Sadie Cohen Print Fund   140:1965

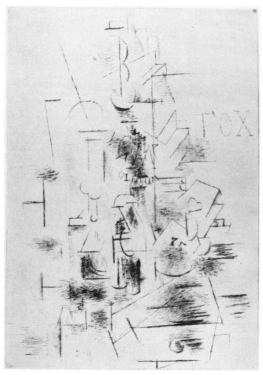

THE ARTIST'S FATHER, 1912
Jacques Villon, French, 1875-1963
Charcoal, 62.9 x 47.6 cm.
Purchase: Funds given by The Measuregraph Co. and
Mr. and Mrs. George S. Rosborough, Jr.   155:1966

THE DINNER TABLE, 1913
Jacques Villon, French, 1875-1963
Drypoint, 28.6 x 38.9 cm.
Purchase 136:1972

VENUS VICTORIOUS, 1915/16, Pierre Auguste Renoir, French, 1841-1919
Bronze, Height: 183.8 cm. Bequest of Curt Valentin 186:1955

ELVIRA RESTING AT A TABLE, 1919
Amedeo Modigliani, Italian, 1884-1920
Oil on canvas, 92.4 x 60.6 cm.
Gift of Joseph Pulitzer, Jr.   77:1968

INTERIOR AT NICE, ca. 1919
Henri Matisse, French, 1869-1954
Oil on canvas, 65.7 x 54.6 cm.
Purchase 74:1945

J. B. NEUMAN, 1919
Ludwig Meidner, German, 1884-1966
Black lithographic crayon, 60.3 x 47.0 cm.
Gift of Mr. and Mrs. Morton D. May   375:1955

STILL LIFE WITH GUITAR, 1920
Juan Gris, Spanish, 1887-1927
Oil on canvas, 50.2 x 61.0 cm.
Purchase 9:1940

THE FIREPLACE, 1916/17
Pablo Picasso, Spanish, 1881-1973
Oil on canvas, 149.2 x 69.9 cm.
Gift of Joseph Pulitzer, Jr.   81:1970

THE BATHER, 1923-25
Jacques Lipchitz, French-American, 1891-1973
Gilt bronze, Height: 197.5 cm.
Gift of Mr. and Mrs. Morton D. May   147:1957

STANDING NUDE, 1918, Joan Miró, Spanish, born 1893, Oil on canvas, 153.1 x 120.7 cm., Purchase: Friends Fund   58:1965

FISHERMEN, 1921
Fernand Léger, French, 1881-1955
Pencil, 26.4 x 37.9 cm.
Purchase: Funds given by
Mrs. John F. Shepley, by exchange   12:1946

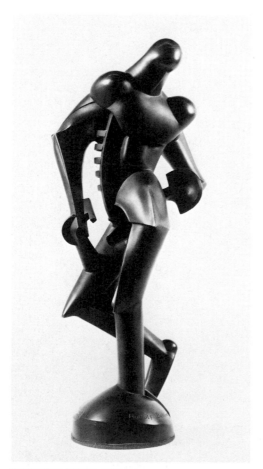

ORGANIC FORM, 1921
Rudolf Belling, German, 1886-1972
Bronze, Height: 54.6 cm.
Gift of Mr. and Mrs. Morton D. May   236:1959

G SMIRG, 1923
Laszlo Moholy-Nagy, Hungarian, 1895-1946
Watercolor and collage, 22.9 x 29.7 cm.
Purchase and Bequest of Horace M. Swope
by exchange   67:1969

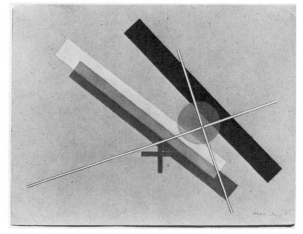

CHRIST AND THE WOMAN TAKEN IN ADULTERY, 1917, Max Beckmann, German, 1884-1950
Oil on canvas, 149.2 x 126.7 cm., Bequest of Curt Valentin   185:1955

EIFFEL TOWER, 1924
Robert Delaunay, French, 1885-1941
Oil on canvas, 160.3 x 95.7 cm.
Gift of Mr. and Mrs. Morton D. May   536:1956

MAN WITH SPECTACLES, 1927-30
Otto Dix, German, 1891-1969
Pastel and watercolor, 47.3 x 30.2 cm.
Gift of Morton D. May   372:1955

ATHLETE IN REPOSE, 1923
Charles Despiau, French, 1874-1946
Bronze, Height: 33.0 cm.
Gift of Joseph Pulitzer, Jr.   119:1969

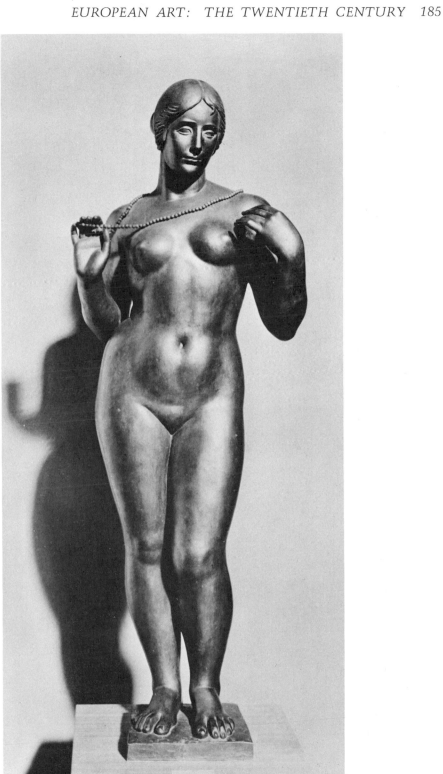

VENUS WITH THE NECKLACE, 1928/29
Aristide Maillol, French, 1861-1944
Bronze, Height: 176.0 cm.
Purchase 1:1941

"TOURBILLONS" VASE, ca. 1925
René Lalique, French, Paris, 1860-1945
Molded and enameled glass, Height: 20.0 cm.
Purchase 63:1930

SIDE CHAIR, 1926
Jacques-Emile Ruhlmann
French, 1879-1933
Macassar ebony, Height: 95.3 cm.
Gift of Mr. and Mrs. Stanley Hanks   110:1972

Left, center
BACCHUS VASE, ca. 1921/22
J. and L. Lobmeyr, Austrian
Blown, wheel-engraved glass, Height: 18.4 cm.
Purchase 17:1927

VASE AND STAND, 1929
Orrefors Glassworks, Swedish
Blown, wheel-engraved glass
Height: 23.5 cm.
Purchase 35:1931

Opposite, detail from
Georges Braque
THE BLUE MANDOLIN 125:1924
See page 191

FOLKE FILBYTER, 1928, Carl Milles, Swedish, 1875-1955, Bronze, Height: 330.0 cm., Purchase 157:1931

FIGURE, 1926-30, Jacques Lipchitz, French-American, 1891-1973
Bronze, Height: 216.6 cm., Gift of Mr. and Mrs. Joseph Pulitzer, Jr.   172:1959

THE BULL FIGHT, 1934
Pablo Picasso, Spanish, 1881-1973
Oil on canvas, 26.7 x 40.7 cm.
Gift of Mr. and Mrs. Marcus Rice   279:1957

THE MINOTAUROMACHY, 1935
Pablo Picasso, Spanish, 1881-1973
Etching, 49.5 x 69.0 cm.
Bequest of Horace M. Swope   665:1940

MANDOLIN AND VASE OF FLOWERS, 1934
Pablo Picasso, Spanish, 1881-1973
Oil on canvas, 80.3 x 99.2 cm.
Purchase 126:1944

SEATED WOMAN, 1953
Pablo Picasso, Spanish, 1881-1973
Oil on canvas, 130.2 x 95.9 cm.
Gift of Joseph Pulitzer, Jr.   196:1953

THE BLUE MANDOLIN, 1930
Georges Braque, French, 1882-1963
Oil on canvas, 115.9 x 87.9 cm.
Purchase 125:1944

SELF PORTRAIT, 1936
Käthe Kollwitz, German, 1867-1945
Bronze, Height: 46.0 cm.
Purchase 8:1942

FAMILY GROUP, 1945
Henry Moore, English, born 1898
Watercolor and crayon, 47.3 x 49.5 cm.
Purchase 95:1947

RECLINING WOMAN, 1932, Henry Moore, English, born 1898, Carved reinforced concrete, Height: 65.1 cm., Purchase 75:1948

SELF PORTRAIT, 1936
Oskar Kokoschka, Austrian, born 1886
Blue crayon, 43.8 x 34.6 cm.
Gift of Mr. and Mrs. Morton D. May   577:1957

WOMAN IN ARMCHAIR, 1936
Henri Matisse, French, 1869-1954
Charcoal, 53.3 x 40.4 cm.
Purchase: Friends Fund   9:1953

THE CHINAMAN, 1938
Georges Rouault, French, 1871-1958
Oil on paper, 63.5 x 48.9 cm.
Gift of Sydney M. Shoenberg, Jr.   580:1958

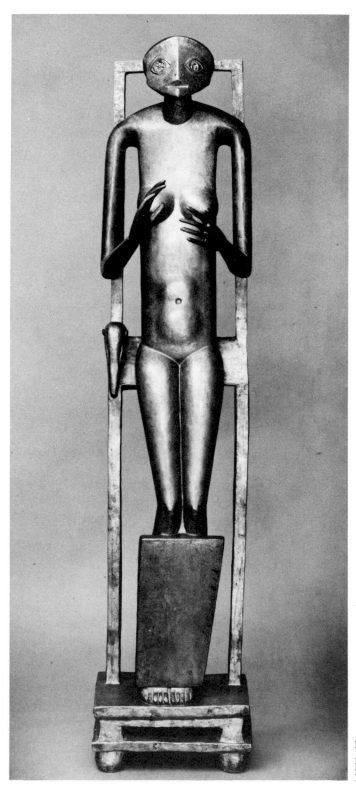

HANDS HOLDING THE VOID, 1934/35
Alberto Giacometti, Swiss, 1901-1966
Bronze, Height: 153.1 cm.
Purchase: Friends Fund   217:1966

THE MAN OF CONFUSION, 1939
Paul Klee, Swiss, 1879-1940
Oil on canvas, 66.7 x 50.5 cm.
Gift of Joseph Pulitzer, Jr.   410:1952

AVIATIC EVOLUTION, 1934
Paul Klee, Swiss, 1879-1940
Oil on canvas, 41.9 x 49.5 cm.
Gift of Morton D. May   233:1954

MOVEMENT AROUND A CHILD
Paul Klee, Swiss, 1879-1940
Watercolor, 20.3 x 30.2 cm.
Purchase: Funds given by
Mrs. Richard K. Weil and by exchange   99:1957

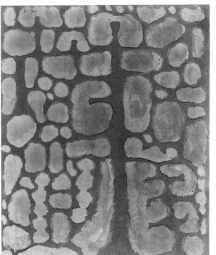

LATE EVENING
LOOKING OUT OF THE WOODS, 1937
Paul Klee, Swiss, 1879-1940
Gouache, 49.5 x 39.4 cm.
Purchase 119:1947

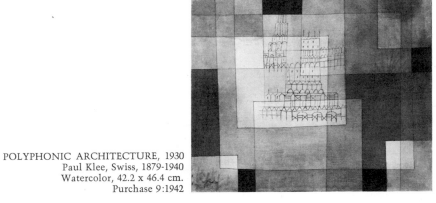

POLYPHONIC ARCHITECTURE, 1930
Paul Klee, Swiss, 1879-1940
Watercolor, 42.2 x 46.4 cm.
Purchase 9:1942

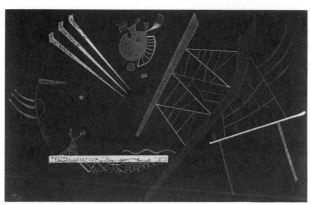

COMPOSITION: GOUACHE ON BLACK, 1940
Wassily Kandinsky, Russian, 1866-1944
Gouache, 32.2 x 49.5 cm.
Purchase: Funds given by Theodore Schempp and
Friends Fund   32:1960

COMPOSITION OF RED AND WHITE, 1938-42
Piet Mondrian, Dutch, 1872-1944
Oil on canvas, 100.3 x 99.1 cm.
Purchase: Friends Fund   242:1972

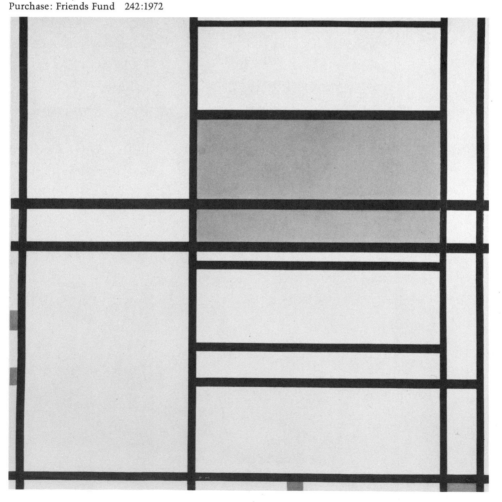

EL GOLEA, 1948
Jean Dubuffet, French, born 1901
Gouache and watercolor, 30.8 x 40.8 cm.
Gift of Joseph Pulitzer, Jr.   33:1952

WALL HANGING: OCEANIE, LA MER
Henri Matisse, French, 1869-1954
Silk screen stencil on linen, 179.4 x 388.9 cm.
Gift of Mr. and Mrs. Anthony Wilson   196:1962

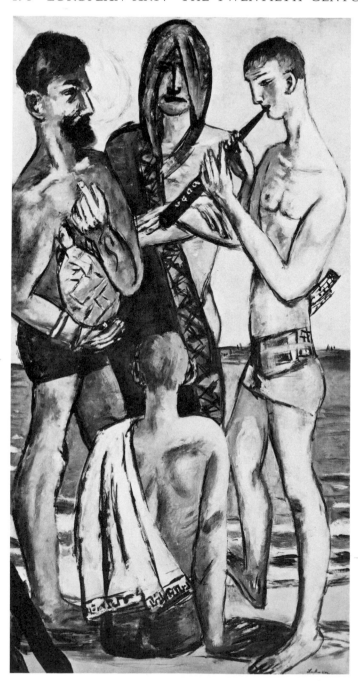

YOUNG MEN BY THE SEA, 1943
Max Beckmann, German, 1884-1950
Oil on canvas, 189.6 x 100.4 cm.
Purchase 106:1946

MASQUERADE, 1948
Max Beckmann, German, 1884-1950
Oil on canvas, 164.6 x 88.2 cm.
Gift of Mr. and Mrs. Joseph Pulitzer, Jr.   587:1958

HORSE AND RIDER, 1949, Marino Marini, Italian, born 1901, Bronze, Height: 179.8 cm., Purchase 171:1955

STILL LIFE, 1953/54
Giorgio Morandi, Italian, 1890-1964
Oil on canvas, 30.5 x 40.2 cm.
Gift of Professor and Mrs. Theo Haimann   230:1957

THE ACTIVE VOICE, 1951
René Magritte, Belgian, 1898-1967
Oil on canvas, 100.3 x 80.0 cm.
Gift of Mr. and Mrs. Joseph Pulitzer, Jr.   4:1960

SMALL RECLINING FIGURE, 1951
Fritz Wotruba, Austrian, born 1907
Bronze, Height: 24.8 cm.
Gift of Mr. and Mrs. Joseph Tucker   25:1964

MAJA, 1942
Gerhard Marcks, German, born 1889
Bronze, Height: 223.6 cm.
Purchase 19:1951

CHEST
Mexican, Olinalá, Guerrero, ca. 1700
Lacquered wood, Height: 60.8 cm.
Gift of Stratford Lee Morton   303:1951

HADLEY TYPE CHEST
Connecticut River Valley, ca. 1680-1710
Oak and pine, Height: 91.4 cm.
Purchase 56:1944

HIGH CHEST, 1730-50
Massachusetts or Connecticut
Walnut veneer, maple
Height: 177.8 cm.
Purchase 158:1929

TANKARD, late 17th-early 18th centuries
John Coney, Boston, 1656-1722
Silver, Height: 17.3 cm.
Purchase: Friends Fund   151:1960

CHAFING DISH, ca. 1730-40
Jacob Hurd, Boston, 1702-1758
Silver, Height: 9.8 cm.
Bequest of Charles H. Stix   62:1948

TEAPOT, ca. 1785
Joseph and Nathaniel Richardson, Philadelphia
Silver, Height: 15.6 cm.
Gift of Charles H. Stix   80:1945

TWO-HANDLED CUPS, 1788
Benjamin Pierpont, Boston, 1730-1797
Engraved silver, Height: 15.1 cm.
Bequest of Charles H. Stix   65, 66:1948

Opposite
COFFEE POT, ca. 1760
Myer Myers, New York, 1723-1795
Silver, Height: 35.2 cm.
Gift of Charles H. Stix   84:1945

SALVERS, 1760-90
Samuel Tingley, New York, active 1767-96
Silver, Diameter: 23.8 cm.
Gift of Charles H. Stix   81, 82:1945

LOW CHEST
Probably Maryland, 1760-90
Mahogany, white pine, Height: 72.4 cm.
Purchase 65:1932

SIDE CHAIR
Philadelphia, 1760-90
Mahogany, Height: 100.3 cm.
Purchase 66:1932

CARD TABLE
Boston area, ca. 1760-90
Mahogany, Height: 71.1 cm.
Purchase 56:1932

BLOCK FRONT CHEST-ON-CHEST, 1767
Probably Boston area
Mahogany, pine, Height: 223.5 cm.
Purchase 183:1929

ANTIOCHUS AND STRATONICE, ca. 1773
Benjamin West, Anglo-American, 1738-1820
Pen, brown ink, white heightening on brown paper
44.9 x 59.5 cm.
Purchase 4:1949

AMERICA PRESENTING AT THE ALTAR
OF LIBERTY MEDALLIONS OF
HER ILLUSTRIOUS SONS
English, ca. 1785
Copperplate printed cotton, Length: 161.3 cm.
Purchase 226:1931

DESK AND BOOKCASE, 1788
Attributed to David Poignand, Boston, 1759-1830
Inlaid mahogany, Height: 249.0 cm.
Bequest of Nellie V. Plant   28:1936

JOANNA AND ELIZABETH PERKINS (?)
Attributed to John Smibert, 1688-1751
Oil on canvas, 63.5 x 76.2 cm.
Gift of Mrs. Daniel K. Catlin   8:1965

SEA CAPTAINS CAROUSING IN SURINAM, John Greenwood, 1727-1792, Oil on bed ticking, 95.9 x 191.2 cm., Purchase 256:1948

THADDEUS BURR, 1758-60
John Singleton Copley
Anglo-American, 1738-1815
Oil on canvas, 128.6 x 101.3 cm.
Purchase 174:1951

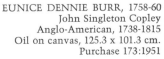

EUNICE DENNIE BURR, 1758-60
John Singleton Copley
Anglo-American, 1738-1815
Oil on canvas, 125.3 x 101.3 cm.
Purchase 173:1951

MAJOR MOSES SEYMOUR, 1789
Ralph Earl, 1751-1801
Oil on canvas, 122.0 x 91.1 cm.
Purchase 34:1948

MRS. MOSES SEYMOUR AND
HER SON, EPAPHRODITUS, 1789
Ralph Earl, 1751-1801
Oil on canvas, 121.8 x 91.5 cm.
Purchase 35:1948

CAPTAIN DAVID COATS
Christian Gullager, 1759-1826
Oil on canvas, 92.7 x 82.0 cm.
Purchase 47:1949

great!

grey –
lace discolored
by age??

MRS. DAVID COATS
Christian Gullager, 1759-1826
Oil on canvas, 93.0 x 82.2 cm.
Purchase 48:1949

STILL LIFE, 1810
John Johnston, 1753-1818
Oil on panel, 37.1 x 46.1 cm.
Anonymous Gift   218:1966

SARAH McCLEAN BOLTON, 1795
Walter Robertson, ca. 1750-1802
Oil on canvas, 76.2 x 62.3 cm.
Purchase 49:1949

TALL CASE CLOCK, ca. 1790-1810
Simon Willard, Roxbury, Massachusetts, 1753-1848
Inlaid mahogany, Height: 221.0 cm.
Purchase 208:1931

MANTLE CLOCK, ca. 1805-10
Dubuc, French, Paris, active 1780-1819
Gilt bronze, Height: 48.5 cm.
Anonymous Gift 52:1970

CANDLESTAND WITH TILT-TOP
Salem, Massachusetts, ca. 1800
Inlaid mahogany, Height: 69.9 cm.
Purchase 42:1931

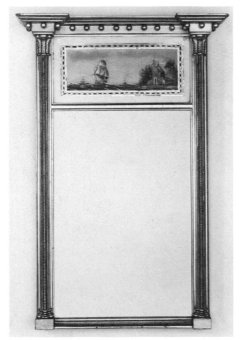

LOOKING GLASS, ca. 1800-10
John Doggett, Roxbury, Massachusetts, 1780-1857
Gilded pine, *eglomisé* panel, Height 90.2 cm.
Purchase: Decorative Arts Society Fund 36:1967

CHAMBER TABLE
Salem, Massachusetts, ca. 1815
Mahogany, white pine, Height: 84.2 cm.
Purchase: Funds given by
Mr. and Mrs. G. Gordon Hertslet 21:1968

SIDE CHAIR
New York, ca. 1800
Mahogany, Height: 82.6 cm.
Purchase 51:1931

CARD TABLE
Boston area, ca. 1805-10
Mahogany, with satinwood and rosewood veneers
Height: 73.7 cm.
Purchase: Funds given by
The family of Judith G. Shepley   116:1971

SIDE TABLE, ca. 1810
Attributed to Henry Connelly
Philadelphia, 1770-1826
Mahogany, mahogany veneers, white marble
Height: 92.7 cm.
Gift of The Measuregraph Company   9:1968

SIDE CHAIRS
Probably New Jersey or New York
Ca. 1815-20
Painted and gilded wood
Height: 83.5 cm.
Purchase 92:1943

THE ADORATION OF THE CHRIST CHILD
Probably Pennsylvania, early 19th century
Embroidered silk, watercolor, 54.0 x 67.3 cm.
Gift of Mrs. William A. McDonnell   17:1972

QUILT, 1807-9
Initialed E.C., printed by John Hewson
Philadelphia, ca. 1745-1821
Pieced and quilted cotton, 295.0 x 285.2 cm.
Purchase 61:1948

SUGAR URN, ca. 1790-1810
Paul Revere, Jr., Boston, 1735-1818
Silver, Height: 21.1 cm.
Purchase 30:1933

TEA CADDY, ca. 1807-10
Anthony Rasch, Philadelphia
Ca. 1778-1858, Silver, Height: 17.9 cm.
Purchase: Decorative Arts Society Fund
And donors   66:1969

TEA SET, ca. 1810
Joel Sayre, New York, 1778-1818
Silver, Height of teapot: 20.0 cm.
Gift of Mr. and Mrs. Milton H. Tucker   81:1968

PITCHER
Probably South Jersey
New Jersey, ca. 1800
Blown, applied glass, Height: 18.7 cm.
Purchase 181:1931

LAURIETTE ASHLEY, ca. 1828, Erastus Salisbury Field, New York, 1805-1900
Oil on canvas, 177.7 x 128.3 cm., Gift of Mrs. James H. Spencer 345:1955

CATSKILL SCENERY
Thomas Cole, 1801-1848
Oil on canvas, 61.6 x 81.9 cm.
Purchase: Friends Fund, Eliza McMillan Fund and
Mrs. John S. Ames and Elizabeth Green by exchange
105:1970

BRIG IN A STORM
Thomas Birch, 1779-1851
Oil on canvas, 42.2 x 59.4 cm.
Purchase 114:1946

THOMAS BIRCH
John Neagle, 1796-1865
Oil on canvas, 76.2 x 63.5 cm.
Purchase: Eliza McMillan Fund   57:1930

COLONEL MENDES COHEN
Rembrandt Peale, 1778-1860
Oil on canvas, 76.2 x 62.3 cm.
Purchase: Eliza McMillan Fund 53:1930

MRS. WILLIAM STEELE, ca. 1820
Samuel L. Waldo, 1783-1861
Oil on panel, 76.2 x 63.5 cm.
Purchase: Eliza McMillan Fund 56:1930

COMPOTES, ca. 1840-50
Boston and Sandwich Glass Co.
Sandwich, Massachusetts, 1825-1888
Pressed glass, Diameter: 26.0 cm.
Bequest of Mrs. Christine Graham Long
435:1961

COMPOTE, ca. 1830-50
Probably Pittsburgh
Pillar molded glass, Height: 27.3 cm.
Bequest of Mrs. Christine Graham Long
446:1961

SUGAR BOWL AND COVER, 1825-40
Attributed to Bakewell, Page & Bakewell
Pittsburgh
Blown, wheel-engraved glass, molded lid
Height: 20.0 cm.
Bequest of Mrs. Christine Graham Long
486:1961

PLATE, ca. 1830-40
Boston and Sandwich Glass Company
Sandwich, Massachusetts, 1825-88
Opaque pressed glass, Diameter: 15.1 cm.
Purchase: Funds given by
Mr. and Mrs. James Myles   51:1971

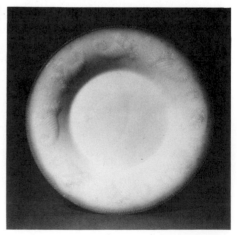

PITCHER, ca. 1832
Factory of William Ellis Tucker
Philadelphia, 1825-38
Overglaze enameled and gilded porcelain
Height: 15.9 cm.
Purchase 29:1971

LIBRARY TABLE, ca. 1850
Alexander Roux, New York, active 1837-81
Rosewood, birch, Height: 74.9 cm.
Purchase: Decorative Arts Society Fund   18:1971

SIDEBOARD
Probably Baltimore, ca. 1825
Mahogany, pine, Height: 132.1 cm.
Purchase: Decorative Arts Society Fund and
Eliza McMillan Fund   26:1971

SOFA TABLE, ca. 1830
Anthony G. Quervelle, Philadelphia, 1789-1856
Rosewood veneer, pine, gilt, marble top, Height: 72.1 cm.
Purchase: Funds given by
Sanford N. and Priscilla R. McDonnell   1:1971

FRIENDSHIP QUILT
Baltimore, 1848
Quilted and appliquéd cotton, 254.0 x 251.5 cm.
Gift of Mrs. Stratford Lee Morton   1:1973
Detail opposite

CASSVILLE, WISCONSIN, 1848
Seth Eastman, 1808-1875
Watercolor, 11.1 x 18.0 cm.
Purchase: Funds given by Lafayette Federal
106:1971

MOONLIGHT VIEW ON THE MISSISSIPPI,
75 MILES ABOVE ST. LOUIS, 1847-49
Seth Eastman, 1808-1875
Watercolor, 11.2 x 17.8 cm.
Purchase: Funds given by various donors   102:1970

TRAVELLING TENTS OF THE SIOUX INDIANS
CALLED A TEPE (sic), 1847-49
Seth Eastman, 1808-1875
Watercolor, 11.2 x 18.0 cm.
Purchase: Funds given by
Western Electric Company   107:1971

BLACK-TAILED HARE, 1841
John James Audubon, 1785-1851
Pencil, chalk, watercolor
40.0 x 57.8 cm.
Purchase 72:1948

CHIEF BILLY BOWLEGS, 1861
Charles F. Wimar, 1828-1862
Oil on canvas, 76.9 x 64.2 cm.
Purchase 9:1938

ATTACK ON
AN EMIGRANT TRAIN, 1854
Charles F. Wimar, 1828-1862
Charcoal, brown ink and
White heightening, 93.4 x 124.5 cm.
Purchase 79:1950

THE WOOD BOAT, 1850
George Caleb Bingham, 1811-1879
Oil on canvas, 62.9 x 75.2 cm.
Purchase 14:1951

SELF PORTRAIT, 1834/35
George Caleb Bingham, 1811-1879
Oil on canvas, 71.2 x 57.2 cm.
Purchase: Eliza McMillan Fund   57:1934

THE JOLLY FLATBOATMEN IN PORT, 1857, George Caleb Bingham, 1811-1879, Oil on canvas, 117.5 x 175.1 cm., Purchase 123:1944

RAFTSMEN PLAYING CARDS, 1847
George Caleb Bingham, 1811-1879
Oil on canvas, 71.2 x 91.5 cm.
Purchase: Ezra H. Linley Fund   50:1934

THE CAPTIVE CHARGER, 1854
Charles F. Wimar, 1828-1862
Oil on canvas, 76.2 x 104.2 cm.
Gift of Lillie B. Randell   181:1925

UPPER MISSISSIPPI, 1855
John F. Kensett, 1816-1872
Oil on canvas, 46.7 x 76.8 cm.
Purchase: Eliza McMillan Fund   22:1950

EAGLE CLIFF, NEW HAMPSHIRE, 1850
Jasper Francis Cropsey, 1823-1900
Oil on canvas, 58.4 x 101.6 cm.
Purchase: Eliza McMillan Fund   18:1950

IN THE ADIRONDACK MOUNTAINS, 1857
William Trost Richards, 1833-1905
Oil on canvas, 77.6 x 100.3 cm.
Bequest of Albert Blair   54:1933

THE HUDSON AT PIERMONT, 1852, Jasper Francis Cropsey, 1823-1900
Oil on canvas, 152.4 x 122.9 cm., Gift of John Allan Love 27:1968

A VASE OF CORN LILIES AND HELIOTROPE, 1863
Martin Johnson Heade, 1819-1904
Oil on canvas, 41.7 x 31.5 cm.
Purchase: Eliza McMillan Fund   68:1965

CHESTER HARDING KRUM, ca. 1858
Chester Harding, 1792-1866
Oil on canvas, 76.2 x 63.5 cm.
Purchase 1133:1940

WOODLAND LANDSCAPE
Asher Brown Durand, 1796-1886
Oil on canvas, 59.7 x 42.8 cm.
Gift of John Allan Love   24:1969

GARDEN BENCH, ca. 1868
Schickle, Harrison and Co.
St. Louis, 1868-1880
Cast iron, Height: 102.2 cm.
Purchase 17:1969

SOFA, New York, ca. 1850-60
Solid and laminated rosewood, Height: 129.5 cm.
Purchase: Friends Fund, Decorative Arts Society Fund
And various donors   95:1972

FAITH
Hiram Powers, 1805-1873
Marble, Height: 71.8 cm.
Gift of J. Harold Pettus   129:1965

PITCHER, ca. 1847/48
Fenton's Works, Bennington, Vermont, 1847-49
Smear-glazed Parian ware, Height: 24.3 cm.
Gift of Miss Stella Koetter   82:1968

SEWING CABINET AND WRITING DESK, ca. 1860-70
Jennens and Bettridge, English, Birmingham, 1816-1864
Lacquered, gilded, painted papier-maché, mother-of-pearl
Height: 39.1 cm., Gift of J. Harold Pettus   130:1965

PEACH BLOW PITCHER, ca. 1880
Hobbs, Brockunier and Company
Wheeling, West Virginia
Blown and cased glass, Height: 18.1 cm.
Purchase 49:1971

HOLLYHOCK AND PEONY WINDOWS, ca. 1885, John LaFarge, 1835-1910
Leaded glass, 221.7 x 94.6 cm., Purchase: Decorative Arts Society Fund 31:1972

SKATING IN CENTRAL PARK, ca. 1860
Winslow Homer, 1836-1910
Pen, brush and watercolor, 41.7 x 62.2 cm.
Purchase: Eliza McMillan Fund   19:1940

THE COUNTRY SCHOOL, 1871
Winslow Homer, 1836-1910
Oil on canvas, 54.3 x 97.5 cm.
Purchase 123:1946

VIEW OF
ST. ANNES RIVER, CANADA, 1870
Robert S. Duncanson, 1817/22-1872
Oil on canvas, 53.3 x 101.6 cm.
Purchase 163:1966

WINONA FALLS, 1877
Alexander H. Wyant, 1836-1892
Oil on canvas, 71.1 x 57.2 cm.
Purchase 24:1915

RUMFORD POINT, MAINE, 1869
Harrison B. Brown, 1831-1915
Oil on canvas, 54.0 x 92.1 cm.
Purchase: Funds given by
Mrs. Arthur Hoskins and
Mr. and Mrs. Warren McK. Shapleigh
4:1965

THE LAND OF EVANGELINE, 1874
Joseph Rusling Meeker, 1827-1889
Oil on canvas, 83.8 x 115.6 cm.
Purchase: Funds given by
Mrs. W. P. Edgerton, by exchange
163:1946

SURVEYOR'S WAGON IN THE ROCKIES
Albert Bierstadt, 1830-1902
Oil on paper on canvas, 19.7 x 32.7 cm.
Gift of J. Lionberger Davis   158:1953

OLEVANO
Albert Bierstadt, 1830-1902
Oil on canvas, 48.6 x 67.3 cm.
Purchase: Eliza McMillan Fund   150:1953

IN THE ROMAN CAMPAGNA, 1873, George Inness, 1825-1894, Oil on panel, 66.1 x 109.2 cm., Purchase 115:1946

WITH THE "STAATS ZEITUNG," 1890
William M. Harnett, 1844/45-1892
Oil on canvas, 35.9 x 51.4 cm.
Purchase 26:1945

THE BRIDGES, FLORENCE
Frank Duveneck, 1848-1919
Oil on canvas, 39.4 x 59.7 cm.
Purchase 26:1921

THE WRECKED SCHOONER, ca. 1903
Winslow Homer, 1836-1910
Watercolor and charcoal, 38.1 x 54.6 cm.
Purchase 25:1938

THE FAIRMAN ROGERS
FOUR-IN-HAND, 1899
Thomas C. Eakins, 1844-1916
Oil on canvas, 59.7 x 90.5 cm.
Purchase 92:1954

THE OUTLAW, 1906
Frederic Remington, 1861-1909
Bronze, Height: 57.2 cm.
Purchase 176:1942

THE BRONCO BUSTER, 1895
Frederic Remington, 1861-1909
Bronze, Height: 58.1 cm.
Gift of J. Lionberger Davis   201:1955

STILL LIFE
William Merritt Chase, 1849-1916
Oil on canvas, 81.3 x 99.1 cm.
Purchase 85:1913

THE TENTH STREET STUDIO, 1880
William Merritt Chase, 1849-1916
Oil on canvas, 91.5 x 122.0 cm.
Bequest of Albert Blair 48:1933

MAUDE SEWING, 1883
F. Childe Hassam, 1859-1935
Watercolor, 35.2 x 25.2 cm.
Bequest of Marie Setz Hertslet   120:1972
Detail opposite

MADISON SQUARE, 1899
Everett Shinn, 1876-1953
Watercolor and chalk, 29.9 x 37.8 cm.
Gift of F. Lee Hawes and Richard S. Hawes III   235:1966

NEW YORK HORSE CAR
Everett Shinn, 1876-1953
Pastel on blue paper, 32.7 x 49.9 cm.
Bequest of Marie Setz Hertslet   124:1972

THE RAINBOW'S SOURCE
John H. Twachtman, 1853-1902
Oil on canvas, 86.7 x 62.2 cm.
Purchase 124:1921

AIR VENT COVER, ca. 1895
Design attributed to Frank Lloyd Wright, 1869-1959
Cast iron, Diameter: 97.5 cm.
Purchase: Funds given by Mr. and Mrs. Stanley Hanks   50:1971

THE PLAZA AFTER RAIN
Paul Cornoyer, 1864-1923
Oil on canvas, 150 x 150 cm.
Purchase 65:1910

BOWL, ca. 1897-1910
Decorated by Ruth Erickson
Grueby Faience and Tile Company, Boston
Opaque enameled, glazed earthenware, Height: 14.0 cm.
Gift of Mr. and Mrs. Stanley Hanks   57:1971

JACK-IN-THE-PULPIT VASE, ca. 1906-12
Tiffany and Co., Corona, New York, 1848-1933
Blown glass, Height: 48.2 cm.
Gift of Miss G. C. Spalding   388:1958

"TRIUMPHAL" VASE, 1904
Taxile Doat, French, 1851-1938
Porcelain, Height: 28.6 cm.
Purchase 334:1911

SECTION OF PORTIERE, ca. 1903
Designed by George W. Maher, 1864-1926
Silk, damask applied on velvet, Height: 200.7 cm.
Purchase 32:1971

SEASHORE, ca. 1910
Maurice B. Prendergast, 1859-1924
Oil on canvas, 60.8 x 81.3 cm.
Purchase: Eliza McMillan Fund 33:1948

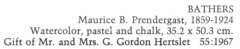

BATHERS
Maurice B. Prendergast, 1859-1924
Watercolor, pastel and chalk, 35.2 x 50.3 cm.
Gift of Mr. and Mrs. G. Gordon Hertslet 55:1967

YOUNG WOMAN IN GREEN, ca. 1915, William J. Glackens, 1870-1938
Oil on canvas, 63.5 x 76.2 cm., Gift of Mr. and Mrs. Ira Glackens 230:1966

WEEHAWKEN, NEW JERSEY, 1910
John Marin, 1870-1953
Watercolor, 47.6 x 39.1 cm.
Bequest of Marie Setz Hertslet   122:1972

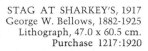

STAG AT SHARKEY'S, 1917
George W. Bellows, 1882-1925
Lithograph, 47.0 x 60.5 cm.
Purchase 1217:1920

HOUSTON STREET, 1917, George Luks, 1867-1933, Oil on canvas, 61.0 x 106.7 cm., Bequest of Marie Setz Hertslet · 121:1972

HEAD OF A WOMAN, 1910-20
Elie Nadelman, 1882-1946
Marble, Height: 36.2 cm.
Gift of J. Lionberger Davis   200:1955

BOATHOUSE, WINTER, HARLEM RIVER, 1918
Ernest Lawson, 1873-1939
Oil on canvas, 63.5 x 76.2 cm.
Bequest of Marie Setz Hertslet   119:1972

STILL LIFE, ca. 1922
Charles Sheeler, 1883-1965
Charcoal, chalk, watercolor, 48.3 x 38.7 cm.
Bequest of Marie Setz Hertslet   123:1972

ROOFTOPS AND FANTASY, 1918
Charles Demuth, 1883-1935
Watercolor, pencil, 25.4 x 35.6 cm.
Gift of Mr. and Mrs. G. Gordon Hertslet   46:1968

BEDROOM, 1922
Yasuo Kuniyoshi, 1893-1953
Pen and ink, 50.2 x 38.7 cm.
Purchase 151:1966

EGGPLANT AND GREEN PEPPER, 1925
Charles Demuth, 1883-1935
Watercolor, pencil, 45.6 x 30.2 cm.
Purchase: Eliza McMillan Fund   2:1948

BOW OF
BEAM TRAWLER OSPREY, 1926
Edward Hopper, 1882-1967
Watercolor, 35.6 x 50.8 cm.
Gift of Mr. and Mrs. G. Gordon Hertslet
1:1972

SULPHUROUS EVENING, 1929, Charles S. Burchfield, 1893-1967
Watercolor, 59.1 x 75.9 cm., Purchase: Eliza McMillan Fund   8:1936

THE GLORIOUS VICTORY OF THE SLOOP MARIA, 1926
Lyonel Feininger, 1871-1956
Oil on canvas, 54.6 x 85.1 cm.
Purchase: Eliza McMillan Fund   848:1940

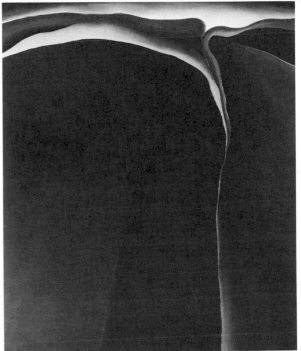

DARK ABSTRACTION, 1924
Georgia O'Keeffe, born 1887
Oil on canvas, 63.2 x 53.0 cm.
Gift of Charles E. and Mary Merrill   187:1955

GAS HOUSE DISTRICT, 1932, Niles Spencer, 1893-1952
Oil on canvas, 76.9 x 102.3 cm.
Purchase and Funds given by Mr. and Mrs. G. Gordon Hertslet   134:1966

DRIFTWOOD ON THE BAGADUCE, 1939-40, Marsden Hartley, 1877-1943
Oil on canvas, 76.6 x 102.0 cm., Gift of Morton D. May   387:1955

STILL LIFE-FEASIBLE #2, 1949-51
Stuart Davis, 1894-1964
Oil on canvas, 30.2 x 41.0 cm.
Gift of Morton D. May   395:1955

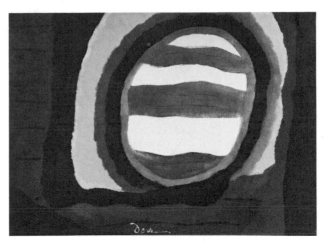

OUT THE WINDOW, 1940
Arthur G. Dove, 1880-1946
Oil on canvas, 38.4 x 53.3 cm.
Purchase 139:1965

SMELT BROOK FALLS, 1937
Marsden Hartley, 1877-1943
Crayon and chalk, 66.0 x 50.2 cm.
Gift of M. Knoedler and Co., Inc.   96:1947

SMELT BROOK FALLS, 1937
Marsden Hartley, 1877-1943
Oil on board, 71.1 x 55.9 cm.
Purchase: Eliza McMillan Fund   9:1939

10 SHOTS 10 CENTS, 1939
Reginald Marsh, 1898-1954
Watercolor, 68.6 x 101.6 cm.
Purchase: Eliza McMillan Fund
41:1941

SWING LOW, SWEET CHARIOT, 1937, John McCrady, born 1911
Oil on canvas, 94.0 x 127.7 cm., Purchase: Eliza McMillan Fund   7:1938

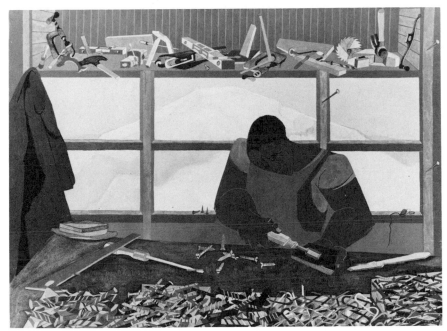

BUILDERS #1, 1972
Jacob Lawrence, born 1917
Watercolor and gouache, 57.2 x 78.1 cm.
Purchase: Eliza McMillan Fund   93:1972

CRADLING WHEAT, 1938
Thomas Hart Benton, 1889-1975
Tempera and oil on board, 78.7 x 96.5 cm.
Purchase 8:1939

COCKFIGHT, 1945
David Smith, 1906-1965
Steel, Height: 114.5 cm.
Purchase 188:1946

WHITE LILY, 1944/45, Alexander Calder, born 1898, Sheet metal and wire, Height: 106.1 cm., Purchase 144:1946

PACIFIC TRANSITION, 1943
Mark Tobey, born 1890
Gouache, 59.1 x 79.4 cm.
Gift of Joseph Pulitzer, Jr. 242:1954

CROUCHING FIGURE, 1935
John Flannagan, 1895-1942
Granite, Height: 39.2 cm.
Gift of Morton D. May 232:1954

A SHADOW ON THE SKY, 1958
Kay Sage, 1898-1963
Watercolor and collage, 62.9 x 45.7 cm.
Gift of Mr. and Mrs. Joseph Pulitzer, Jr. 5:1960

UNTITLED, 1958
Sam Francis, American, born 1923
Oil on canvas, 191.5 x 105.4 cm.
Anonymous Gift   245:1962

ASHEVILLE, 1948
Willem de Kooning, American, born 1904
Sapolin, 48.3 x 61.0 cm.
Purchase 150:1966

TEXTUROLOGIE XXXI, 1958
Jean Dubuffet, French, born 1901
Oil on canvas, 114.0 x 145.4 cm.
Gift of Mr. and Mrs. Joseph Pulitzer, Jr.   51:1967

MARRIAGE OF REASON AND SQUALOR, 1959, Frank Stella, American, born 1936
Oil on canvas, 229.9 x 334.1 cm., Purchase and Funds given by Mr. and Mrs. Joseph A. Helman, Mr. and Mrs. Ronald K. Greenberg   23:1969

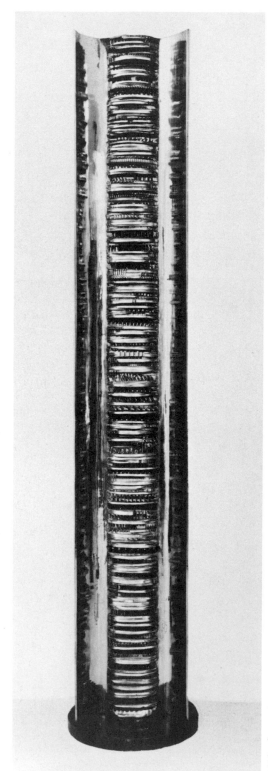

KALOTA, 1963
Victor de Vasarely, Hungarian, born 1908
Oil on canvas, 200.0 x 209.9 cm.
Purchase: Funds given by Henry B. Pflager and the Shoenberg Foundation   5:1965

Opposite
RED, ORANGE, ORANGE ON RED, 1962
Mark Rothko, American, 1903-1970
Oil on canvas, 233.7 x 204.5 cm.
Purchase: Funds given by the Shoenberg Foundation   129:1966

TRAVELER'S COLUMN, 1960-65
Arnaldo Pomodoro, Italian, born 1926
Bronze, Height: 261.7 cm.
Purchase 137:1965

DRIVE, 1965
Kenneth Noland, American, born 1924
Acrylic on canvas, 176.5 x 176.5 cm.
Purchase 149:1966

ALPHA-TAU, 1961, Morris Louis, American, 1912-1962, Acrylic on canvas, 259.1 x 594.5 cm., Purchase: Funds given by The Shoenberg Foundation 8:1968

SPECTRUM II, 1966/67
Ellsworth Kelly, American, born 1923
Oil on canvas, 203.2 x 693.6 cm.
Purchase: Funds given by the Shoenberg Foundation   4:1967

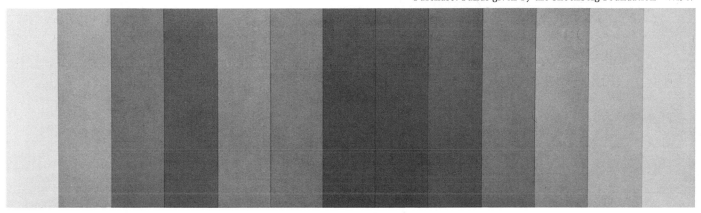

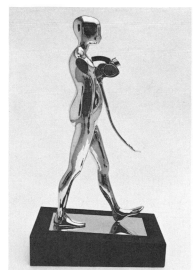

STUDY: FALLING MAN (WALKING MAN), 1964
Ernest Trova, American, born 1927
Chrome plated bronze, Height: 152.4 cm.
Gift of Morton D. May   28:1967

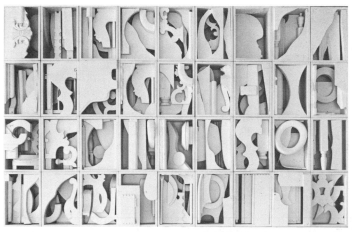

NEW CONTINENT, 1962
Louise Nevelson, American, born 1900
Wood, Width: 309.3 cm.
Purchase and funds given by various donors   14:1967

TRI LEVEL I, 1970/71, Ron Davis, American, born 1937, Fiberglass, 127.0 x 355.7 cm.
Purchase: Funds given by National Endowment for the Arts and Contemporary Art Society Fund 28:1971

TUBE BEING STEPPED ON, 1969
Claes Oldenburg, American, born 1929
Watercolor, crayon and pencil, 34.6 x 27.9 cm.
Purchase: Contemporary Art Society Fund   41:1969

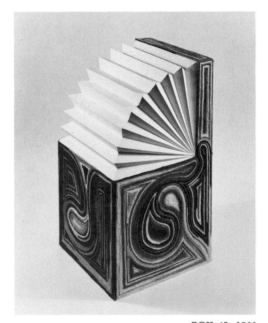

DRAWING F, 1966
Lucas Samaras, American, born 1936
Pencil, 42.9 x 35.6 cm.
Gift of Mr. and Mrs. Joseph L. Tucker
83:1969

BOX 45, 1966
Lucas Samaras, American, born 1936
Wood, wool and paint, Height: 55.9 cm.
Purchase: Funds given by
Mr. and Mrs. George H. Schlapp
2:1967

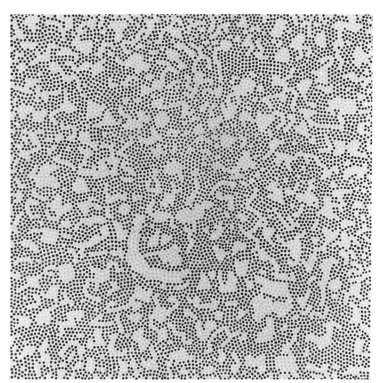

#21, 1968
Peter Young, American, born 1940
Acrylic on canvas, 241.4 x 241.4 cm.
Purchase: Contemporary Art Society Fund
247:1972

UNTITLED, 1965
Bruce Nauman, American, born 1941
Fiberglass, Height: 208.3 cm.
Purchase: Funds given by
National Endowment for the Arts and
Contemporary Art Society Fund   27:1971

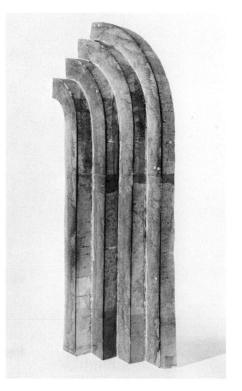

CATHEDRAL #3, 1969
Roy Lichtenstein
American, born 1923
Color lithograph, 123.2 x 82.6 cm.
Purchase: Sidney and Sadie Cohen
Print Fund   43:1969.3

CONFLUENCE, 1964/65
Masayuki Nagare, Japanese, born 1923
Granite, Height: 81.3 cm.
Gift of Mr. and Mrs. Howard F. Baer   16:1964

GIANT 3-WAY PLUG "CUBE TAP," 1970/71
Claes Oldenburg, American, born 1929
Cor-Ten steel and bronze, Length: 294.7 cm.
Gift of the Shoenberg Foundation   21:1971

PRAISE FOR ELOHIM ADONAI, 1966, Mark di Suvero, American, born 1933
Wood and steel, Height: 670.7 cm., Gift of Mr. and Mrs. Norman B. Champ, Jr.   31:1967

UNTITLED, 1969, Donald Judd, American, born 1928
Anodized aluminum and blue Plexiglas, 121 x 152 x 723 cm., Gift of the Shoenberg Foundation   1:1970

MONSTER MASK, T'AO T'IEH, 11th-10th century B.C., Western Chou Dynasty, 1027-771 B.C.
Bronze, Width: 41.9 cm., Purchase 288:1949

CONTAINER, FANG I
16th-15th century B.C.
Bronze, Height: 21.3 cm.
Gift of J. Lionberger Davis   127:1951

WINE GOBLET, KU
16th-15th century B.C.
Bronze, Height: 21.7 cm.
Gift of J. Lionberger Davis   29:1951

FOOD COOKING VESSEL, FANG TING
14th-11th century B.C.
Bronze, Height: 21.3 cm.
Gift of J. Lionberger Davis   222:1950

FOOD COOKING VESSEL, FANG TING
14th-11th century B.C.
Bronze, Height: 23.3 cm.
Gift of Miss Leona J. Beckmann   108:1954

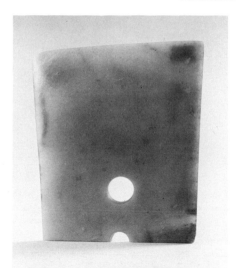

RITUAL BLADE, TSI
Green jade, Height: 17.5 cm.
Purchase: W. K. Bixby Fund   204:1920

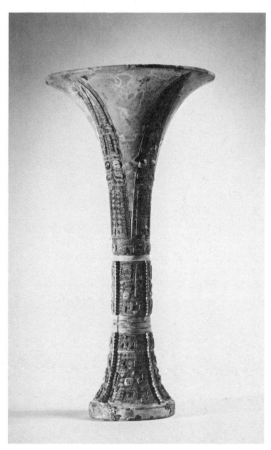

WINE GOBLET, KU
12th-11th century B.C.
Bronze, Height: 32.7 cm.
Gift of J. Lionberger Davis   217:1950

RITUAL BLADE, TSI
Green jade, Length: 11.6 cm.
Purchase 87:1917

WINE HEATING VESSEL, CHIA
12th-11th century B.C.
Bronze, Height: 34.0 cm.
Gift of J. Lionberger Davis   224:1950

FOOD CONTAINER, KUEI
Western Chou, 11th-10th century B.C.
Bronze, Height: 21.3 cm.
Gift of J. Lionberger Davis   123:1951

WINE CONTAINER, YU
Western Chou, 11th-10th century B.C.
Bronze, Height: 26.7 cm.
Gift of J. Lionberger Davis   225:1950

WATER CONTAINER, CHIH
Western Chou, 11th-10th century B.C.
Bronze, Height: 14.7 cm.
Gift of J. Lionberger Davis   215:1950

FOOD COOKING VESSEL, CHIA
Western Chou, 11th-10th century B.C.
Bronze, Height: 45.9 cm.
Gift of J. Lionberger Davis   221:1950

WINE CONTAINER, FANG LEI, Western Chou, 11th-10th century B.C., Bronze, Height: 62.7 cm., Purchase 2:1941

WATER CONTAINER, I
Late Western-early Eastern Chou
9th-7th century B.C.
Bronze, Length: 38.4 cm.
Gift of J. Lionberger Davis   213:1950

WINE CONTAINER, HU
Western Chou, 9th century B.C.
Bronze, Height: 53.7 cm.
Purchase 281:1948

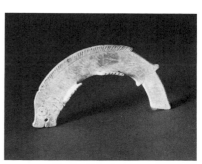

PENDANT IN THE FORM OF A FISH
Eastern Chou, 7th-3rd century B.C.
Calcified jade, Length: 10.2 cm.
Gift of J. Lionberger Davis   484:1956

RITUAL CYLINDER, TS'UNG
Late Western-early Eastern Chou
10th-7th century B.C.
Calcified jade, Diameter: 8.0 cm.
Purchase 136:1919

Detail from Chinese Village shown below

TOMB TILE, PART OF A GABLE
Stamped, painted, grey earthenware, Height: 79.9 cm.
Purchase: Funds given by John M. Olin Trust   57:1953

A SIMULATED CHINESE VILLAGE, Tomb figures, principally from the Han Dynasty, Earthenware, Gift of the heirs of Berenice Ballard 104:1950

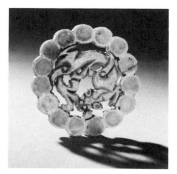

RITUAL DISK, PI
3rd century B.C.
Green jade, Diameter: 23.7 cm.
Purchase 92:1917

APPLIQUE OR PENDANT
Glass, Diameter: 5.5 cm.
Gift of J. Lionberger Davis 490:1956

GIANT PANDA, Gilt bronze, Height: 13.7 cm., Purchase 35:1933

TOMB FIGURE, STANDING FEMALE
Polychromed earthenware, Height: 30.7 cm.
Purchase 46:1949

MODEL OF A FOWLING TOWER
Glazed earthenware, Height: 62.4 cm.
Purchase: W. K. Bixby Fund   131:1947

"HILL" JAR
Green glazed earthenware, Height: 26.0 cm.
Purchase 266:1919

FINIAL, ANTELOPE
Ordos region
Bronze, Height: 16.2 cm.
Purchase: W. K. Bixby Fund   28:1943

POLETOP, WILD ASS
Ordos region
Bronze, Height: 17.9 cm.
Purchase: W. K. Bixby Fund   30:1943

RELIEF PLAQUE OF A TIGER
Ordos region
Bronze, Width: 17.3 cm.
Purchase: W. K. Bixby Fund   19:1943

BUCKLE FROM CHAIN
Ordos region
Bronze, Length: 10.9 cm.
Gift of Mr. and Mrs. Alvin S. Novack   73:1957

Opposite
CASKET AND LOCK
T'ang Dynasty, 618-907
Glazed earthenware, bronze lock
Height: 12.7 cm.
Bequest of Samuel C. Davis   931:1940

STELE: SAKYAMUNI TRIAD, 505, Northern Wei Dynasty, 386-535
Grey limestone, Height: 188.0 cm., Purchase 38:1936

BODHISATTVA, AVALOKITESVARA
KUAN YIN
Early 6th century
Northern Wei Dynasty, 386-535
Gilt bronze, Height: 14.8 cm.
Purchase 4:1942

BODHISATTVA, MAITREYA, MI-LO
Northern Ch'i Dynasty, 550-577
Gilt bronze, Height: 13.3 cm.
Purchase 145:1946

BUDDHA
Sui Dynasty, 581-618
Marble, Height: 191.8 cm.
Purchase 182:1919

HORSE AND RIDER
Gilt bronze, enamel, Length: 11.4 cm.
Gift of C. T. Loo   38:1941

PAIR OF DIGNITARIES
Glazed earthenware, Height: 57.7 cm.
Bequest of Samuel C. Davis   924:1940

BODHISATTVA, AVALOKITESVARA, KUAN YIN
8th Century
Gilt bronze, Height: 27.9 cm.
Purchase 36:1933

LAMP
Glazed earthenware, Height: 7.8 cm.
Bequest of Samuel C. Davis 930:1940

EWER
Brown glazed earthenware, Height: 16.1 cm.
Purchase 289:1949

SHALLOW BOWL
Glazed earthenware, Diameter: 21.6 cm.
Purchase 3:1927

BACTRIAN CAMEL
Glazed earthenware, Height: 86.6 cm.
Purchase: W. K. Bixby Fund
181:1942

TRIPOD DISH
Glazed earthenware, Diameter: 28.7 cm.
Bequest of Samuel C. Davis   935:1940

JAR
Glazed earthenware
Height: 18.7 cm.
Purchase 4:1927

COVERED JAR
Glazed earthenware, Height: 26.6 cm.
Purchase: W. K. Bixby Fund   177:1942

FLASK
Glazed earthenware
Height: 22.5 cm.
Bequest of Samuel C. Davis
925:1940

COVERED JAR
Blue and white glazed earthenware
Height: 22.2 cm.
Purchase 18:1951

JAR
Blue glazed earthenware
Height: 15.1 cm.
Purchase: W. K. Bixby Fund
68:1952

TRIPOD DISH
Amber and brown glazed earthenware
Diameter: 12.8 cm.
Gift of J. Lionberger Davis   115:1965

PERFORMING HORSE AND RIDER
Grey earthenware, Height: 58.4 cm.
Purchase 59:1941

TEA BOWL, TING WARE
Brown glazed porcelain, Diameter: 11.2 cm.
Bequest of Samuel C. Davis   1005:1940

CUP STAND, "RED" TING WARE
Brown glazed porcelain
Height: 6.0 cm.
Bequest of Samuel C. Davis
1006:1940

BOWL, TING WARE
Brown glazed porcelain, copper rim
Diameter: 16.7 cm.
Bequest of Samuel C. Davis   998:1940

BOWL, TING WARE
12th-13th century
Glazed porcelain, copper rim
Diameter: 20.5 cm.
Bequest of Samuel C. Davis   979:1940

BODHISATTVA, AVALOKITESVARA, KUAN YIN, Polychromed wood, Height: 99.2 cm., Purchase 110:1947

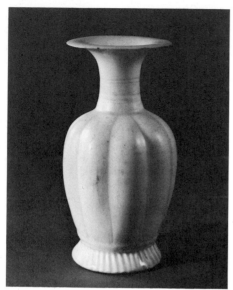

VASE, CH'ING PAI / YING-CH'ING WARE
Early 12th century
Celadon glazed porcelain, Height: 17.4 cm.
Bequest of Samuel C. Davis   1121:1940

TABLE ORNAMENT
SHEEP, LION AND FUNGUS
12th century
Amber and brown jade, Length: 6.8 cm.
Purchase 134:1919

"CHAMPION" VASE
12th-13th century
Greyish white jade, Height: 9.2 cm.
Purchase: W. K. Bixby Fund   202:1920

DISH, JU WARE
Early 12th century
Celadon glazed stoneware, Diameter: 17.2 cm.
Bequest of Samuel C. Davis   973:1940

MEI-P'ING VASE
CH'ING PAI / YING CH'ING WARE
Early 12th century
Celadon glazed porcelain, Height: 34.6 cm.
Bequest of Samuel C. Davis   940:1940

PILLOW, TZ'U CHOU WARE, 12th century
Glazed slip painted stoneware, Width: 20.0 cm.
Purchase: W. K. Bixby Fund   290:1949

MEI-P'ING VASE, TZ'U CHOU WARE
12th century
Glazed slip painted stoneware, Height: 31.3 cm.
Bequest of Samuel C. Davis   949:1940

MEI-P'ING VASE, TZ'U CHOU WARE, 11th century
Glazed slip painted stoneware, Height: 41.0 cm.
Bequest of Samuel C. Davis   945:1940

MEI-P'ING VASE, TZ'U CHOU WARE
12th century
Glazed slip painted stoneware, Height: 30.3 cm.
Bequest of Samuel C. Davis   946:1940

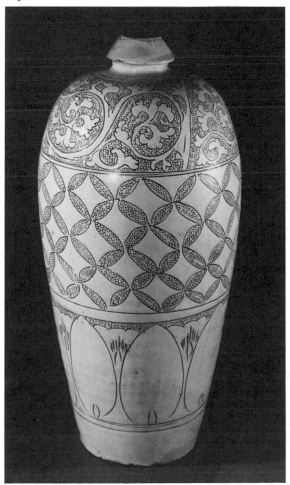

BOWL, "HANGCHOW" WARE
Celadon glazed porcelain
Diameter: 16.5 cm.
Gift of Mrs. I. D. Kelley
269:1951

TEXTILE FRAGMENT, HANDSCROLL COVER
Silk, *K'o-ssu*, tapestry weave, 26.8 x 19.3 cm.
Purchase 97:1926

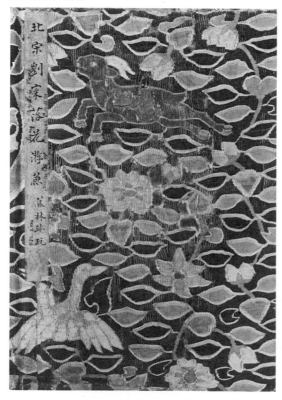

INCENSE JAR, KUAN WARE
Grey celadon glazed stoneware
Copper rim, Height: 9.6 cm.
Bequest of Samuel C. Davis   1076:1940

TRIPOD INCENSE JAR, LUNG CH'UAN WARE
Celadon glazed stoneware, Diameter: 13.3 cm.
Purchase 249:1919

FISH SWIMMING AMID FALLING FLOWERS
Traditionally attributed to Liu Ts'ai, active 1068-85
Ink and color on silk, 26.4 x 252.2 cm.
Purchase: W. K. Bixby Fund   97:1926

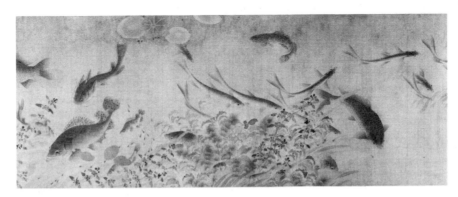

THE ELEVENTH LOHAN, 14th century
Ink and color on silk, 126.0 x 62.2 cm.
Purchase 851:1920

VASE, LUNG CH'UAN WARE, early 14th century
Celadon glazed porcelain, Height: 72.4 cm.
Bequest of Samuel C. Davis   942:1940

SEAL INK BOX, TZ'U CHOU WARE
Clear glazed slip painted stoneware
Diameter: 9.0 cm.
Bequest of Samuel C. Davis   915:1940

MEI-P'ING VASE, TZ'U CHOU WARE
Late 13th century
Slip painted stoneware under blue glaze
Height: 26.8 cm.
Bequest of Mrs. R. L. Metcalfe   56:1918

JAR, TZ'U CHOU WARE
Late 13th century
Clear glazed slip painted stoneware
Overglaze enamels, Height: 30.9 cm.
Bequest of Samuel C. Davis   944:1940

MEI-P'ING VASE, TZ'U CHOU WARE
1st half 14th century
Clear glazed slip painted stoneware
Height: 40.3 cm.
Gift of C. T. Loo   9:1937

BULB BOWL, CHUN WARE
Glazed stoneware, Diameter: 20.3 cm.
Bequest of Samuel C. Davis   988:1940

BULB BOWL, CHUN WARE
Glazed stoneware, Diameter: 20.0 cm.
Bequest of Samuel C. Davis   987:1940

VESSEL IN ARCHAIC KUEI FORM
Ming Dynasty, 14th-15th century
Grey jade mottled with brown
Width: 18.3 cm.
Purchase 186:1916

MEI-P'ING VASE, TZ'U CHOU WARE
14th century
Glazed stoneware, Height: 27.9 cm.
Bequest of Samuel C. Davis   947:1940

JAR, TZ'U CHOU WARE, 14th century
Brown glazed stoneware, Height: 33.1 cm.
Gift of C. T. Loo   835:1920

BOWL
Mark and period of Hung Chih, 1488-1505
Clear glazed white porcelain, Diameter: 19.6 cm.
Gift of J. Lionberger Davis 210:1955

COVERED BOX
Mark and period of Yung-Lo, 1403-24
Cinnebar lacquer, Diameter: 5.5 cm.
Gift of J. Lionberger Davis 493:1956

COVERED BOX
Mark and period of Hsüan-Tê, 1426-35
Cinnebar lacquer, Diameter: 10.1 cm.
Purchase 63:1917

TWO TAOIST FIGURES, LUNG CH'UAN WARE
Late 14th-early 15th century
Celadon glazed porcelain, Height: 24.4 cm.
Bequest of Samuel C. Davis 936:1940

JAR, FA HUA WARE
Late 15th century
Enamel glazed porcelain, Height: 18.8 cm.
Bequest of Samuel C. Davis 1108:1940

SCRAP BOWL
Mark and period of Chia Ching, 1522-66
Underglaze blue and overglaze enameled porcelain
Height: 7.2 cm.
Bequest of Samuel C. Davis   1074:1940

SCRAP BOWL
Mark and period of Chia Ching, 1522-66
Enamels on porcelain biscuit, Height: 7.2 cm.
Gift of J. Lionberger Davis   208:1955

STEM CUP
Chia Ching period, 1522-66
Cinnebar lacquer, yellow ground, silver liner
Height: 11.4 cm., Diameter: 15.9 cm.
Purchase 83:1923

JAR
Mark and period of Chia Ching, 1522-66
Overglaze enameled porcelain, Height: 13.8 cm.
Purchase: W. K. Bixby Fund   280:1952

Opposite
DETAIL FROM A TEXTILE FRAGMENT
16th century
Silk, compound weave, 54.0 x 88.9 cm.
Bequest of William Corman   9:1958

BOWL
Mark and period of Chia Ching, 1522-66
Underglaze blue and overglaze red enameled
Porcelain, Diameter: 36.8 cm.
Purchase 36:1936

CHAIR COVER, 17th century
Silk, *K'o-ssu*, tapestry weave, 158.1 x 47.6 cm.
Gift of Mrs. Samuel C. Davis   86:1941

BOATING ON THE RIVER ON A SNOWY NIGHT
Early 16th century
Ink and color on silk, 121.9 x 66.0 cm.
Purchase 855:1920

GUARDIAN LION, K'ang Hsi Period, 1662-1722, Enamels on porcelain biscuit, Height: 53.6 cm., Purchase 31:1917

VASE
K'ang Hsi Period, 1662-1722
Enamels on porcelain biscuit
Height: 26.0 cm.
Bequest of Samuel C. Davis   1099:1940

VASE
K'ang Hsi Period, 1662-1722
Overglaze enameled porcelain
Height: 38.7 cm.
Purchase 138:1915

PAIR OF VASES
K'ang Hsi Period, 1662-1722
Overglaze enameled porcelain
Height: 48.3 cm.
Gift of Mrs. H. Lionel Herzfelder   60:1962

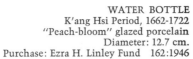

WATER BOTTLE
K'ang Hsi Period, 1662-1722
"Peach-bloom" glazed porcelain
Diameter: 12.7 cm.
Purchase: Ezra H. Linley Fund   162:1946

WINE POT, TE-HUA WARE
Late 17th-early 18th century
Glazed porcelain, Height: 15.1 cm.
Bequest of Samuel C. Davis   1041:1940

SEAL INK BOX
Mark and period of K'ang Hsi, 1662-1722
"Peach-bloom" glazed porcelain
Diameter: 7.3 cm.
Gift of J. Lionberger Davis   212:1955

VASE
Mark and period of K'ang Hsi, 1662-1722
"Peach-bloom" glazed porcelain
Height: 15.6 cm.
Gift of J. Lionberger Davis   211:1955

BRUSH WASHER
Mark and period of K'ang Hsi, 1662-1722
Underglaze red and blue decorated porcelain
Height: 7.2 cm.
Bequest of Samuel C. Davis   1066:1940

BOTTLE
K'ang Hsi Period, 1662-1722
Lang-yao glazed porcelain, Height: 28.4 cm.
Purchase 40:1919

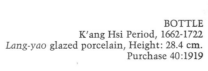

RHYTON, 18th century
Pale yellow-green jade, Height: 19.8 cm.
Purchase 120:1919

WATER BOTTLE
Ch'ien Lung Period, 1736-95
"Lavender-blue" glazed porcelain, Height: 12.4 cm.
Bequest of Samuel C. Davis 1051:1940

CABBAGE VASE, TE-HUA WARE
Ch'ien Lung Period, 1736-95
Glazed porcelain, Height: 15.4 cm.
Gift of Draper and Draper 63:1943

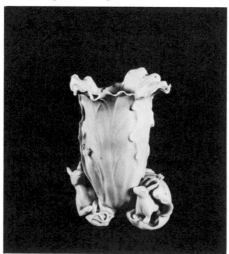

COVERED VASE
Ch'ien Lung Period, 1736-95
White jadeite, Height: 33.0 cm.
Purchase 122:1919

BUDDHA WITH TWO DISCIPLES
From a set of thirteen *tankas* illustrating Jataka Tales
Tibetan, 18th century
Color on prepared cotton, 86.0 x 54.0 cm.
Purchase: W. K. Bixby Fund 193:1950

ENJOYMENT OF CHRYSANTHEMUM FLOWERS, 1753
Hua Yen, 1680-1755
Ink and color on paper, 64.5 x 114.8 cm.
Purchase: W. K. Bixby Fund 7:1954

HANGING OR COVER, Ch'ien Lung Period, 1736-95
Silk, *K'o-ssu*, tapestry weave, 301.4 x 274.0 cm., Purchase: W. K. Bixby Fund   74:1956

**SAUCER WITH ARMS OF
THE DUKE OF ANHALT**
For the German market, ca. 1750
Overglaze enameled porcelain, Diameter: 16.5 cm.
Gift of the Winfield Foundation   161:1955

EWER
For the European market, ca. 1700-15
Overglaze enameled porcelain, Height: 27.5 cm.
Purchase: Funds given by various donors   30:1971

SMALL TUREEN
For the Dutch market, ca. 1725-50
Overglaze enameled porcelain, Diameter: 20.1 cm.
Gift of the Winfield Foundation 163:1955

DISH WITH ARMS OF SALDANHA DE ALBUQUERQUE
For the Portuguese market, ca. 1760-70
Overglaze enameled porcelain, Diameter: 22.4 cm.
Gift of the Winfield Foundation   142:1955

SOUP PLATE
For the Danish market (?), ca. 1760-70
Overglaze enameled porcelain, Diameter: 23.2 cm.
Gift of the Winfield Foundation   120:1955

SOUP PLATE
For the European market, ca. 1760-70
Overglaze enameled, gilded porcelain
Diameter: 23.0 cm.
Gift of the Winfield Foundation   67:1955

PLATTER WITH ARMS OF GORDON
For the Scottish market, ca. 1780
Underglaze blue, overglaze enameled, gilded porcelain
Length: 36.8 cm.
Gift of the Winfield Foundation   106:1955

PLATE, GREEN "FITZHUGH" PATTERN
For the American market, ca. 1810
Overglaze enameled porcelain
Diameter: 19.4 cm.
Gift of the Winfield Foundation   154:1955

PLATTER WITH ARMS OF ARAUJO DE ACEBEDO
For the Portuguese market, ca. 1785-1800
Overglaze enameled porcelain, Length: 29.5 cm.
Gift of the Winfield Foundation   112:1955

PLATTER, ORANGE "FITZHUGH" PATTERN
For the English or American market, ca. 1790-1820
Overglaze enameled and gilded porcelain, Length: 47.8 cm.
Gift of the Winfield Foundation   150:1955

MUSICIAN, SHO PLAYER, ca. 1100
Lacquered and gilded wood, Height: 26.0 cm.
Purchase: W. K. Bixby Fund   146:1959

SHINTO GODDESS, 9th-10th century
Wood with *kirigane*, polychrome, Height: 20.3 cm.
Purchase: W. K. Bixby Fund   69:1965

JAR, TOKONAME WARE
Late 12th-early 13th century
Ash-glazed stoneware, Height: 22.5 cm.
Purchase: W. K. Bixby Fund   57:1963

DESCENT OF AMIDA BUDDHA, 13th century
Ink, color and *kirigane* on silk, 97.6 x 39.4 cm.
Purchase: Friends Fund   20:1961

MONJU BOSATSU ON HIS LION, 13th century
Ink and color on silk, 106.0 x 55.2 cm.
Purchase: Friends Fund   21:1961

FUDO-MYOO, 1st half 13th century
Lacquered wood with polychrome and *kirigane*
Height: 52.4 cm., Purchase: Funds given by
The Jordan Charitable Foundation 100:1972

STANDING BUDDHA
Late 12th-early 13th century
Lacquered, polychromed and gilded wood, Height: 82.6 cm.
Purchase 132:1966

BOTTLE, BIZEN WARE
Muromachi Period, 15th-16th century
Ash-glazed stoneware, Height: 23.2 cm.
Purchase: W. K. Bixby Fund   59:1963

WRITING CASE, SUZURI-BAKO
Muromachi Period, 15th century
Lacquered wood, Width: 22.3 cm.
Purchase: W. K. Bixby Fund and the
Beatrice T. Hoskins Trust   245:1972

STORAGE JAR, TAMBA WARE
Momoyama Period, ca. 1600
Ash-glazed stoneware, Height: 39.4 cm.
Purchase: W. K. Bixby Fund   58:1963

WINE BOTTLE, KO-IMARI WARE, ca. 1615-43
Underglaze blue decorated porcelain, Height: 20.8 cm.
Purchase: Friends Fund   13:1960

PLATE, KO-IMARI WARE, ca. 1615-43
Underglaze blue decorated porcelain
Diameter: 19.7 cm.
Purchase: Funds given anonymously   60:1963

HAND WARMER, KO-IMARI WARE
2nd half 17th century
Underglaze blue and overglaze enameled
Porcelain, Height: 14.2 cm.
Purchase: W. K. Bixby Fund   143:1959

BOWL, KO-IMARI WARE, ca. 1615-43
Underglaze blue decorated porcelain
Diameter: 39.5 cm.
Purchase: W. K. Bixby Fund   342:1962

OCTAGONAL BOWL, "KAKIEMON" WARE
For export to Europe, late 17th-early 18th century
Overglaze enameled porcelain, Diameter: 25.5 cm.
Purchase: W. K. Bixby Fund and funds given by
Mr. and Mrs. Arthur B. Baer   49:1970

DISH, KO-IMARI WARE
For export to Europe, ca. 1680
Underglaze blue, overglaze enameled and gilded porcelain
Diameter: 31.0 cm.
Purchase: W. K. Bixby Fund   56:1962

JAR, KO-IMARI WARE
For export to Europe, second half 17th century
Overglaze enameled porcelain, Height: 29.9 cm.
Purchase: Funds given by Mr. and Mrs. Arthur B. Baer
75:1968

LARGE DISH, KO-IMARI WARE
Made for the Dutch East India Company, ca. 1658-83
Underglaze blue decorated porcelain, Diameter: 39.0 cm.
Purchase: W. K. Bixby Fund   14:1969

DISH, NABESHIMA WARE, late 17th century
Underglaze blue and overglaze enameled
porcelain, Diameter: 15.6 cm.
Purchase: W. K. Bixby Fund   142:1959

EWER, NABESHIMA WARE, ca. 1736-43
Underglaze blue decorated porcelain
Height: 17.9 cm.
Purchase: Funds given by
The Jordan Charitable Foundation   101:1972

DISH, MATSUGATANI OR
NABESHIMA WARE
Late 17th century
Underglaze blue decorated porcelain
Length: 16.9 cm.
Purchase   114:1969

Opposite, detail from
HORSES IN STABLES, 4:1970
See pages 314-315

PLATE, "KAKIEMON" WARE, early 18th century
Underglaze blue decorated porcelain, Diameter: 21.5 cm.
Purchase: W. K. Bixby Fund   32:1969

LARGE DISH, AO-KUTANI WARE, late 17th-early 18th century
Overglaze enameled porcelain, Diameter: 38.1 cm.
Purchase: Funds given by Mr. and Mrs. Arthur B. Baer   148:1966

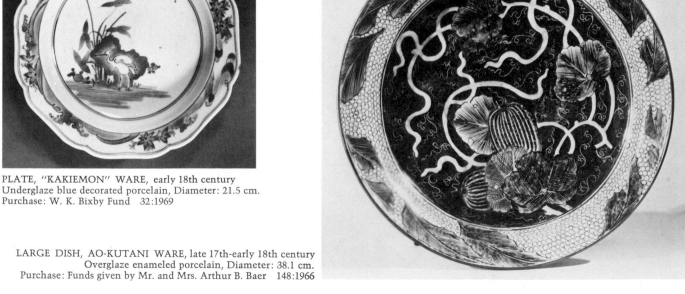

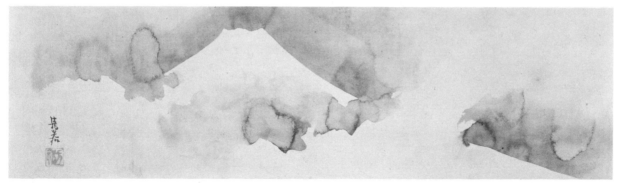

FUJIYAMA
Ogata Korin, 1663-1743
Ink on paper, 24.0 x 85.0 cm.
Purchase: Friends Fund   58:1962

AUTUMN LEAVES AND GRASSES, ca. 1850
Shibata Zeshin, 1807-1891
Lacquer on paper, mica ground, 15.0 x 46.0 cm.
Purchase: Friends Fund   15:1960

HORSES IN STABLES, SPRING AND AUTUMN
Pair of six-fold screens, 17th century
Ink, color, gold, silver on paper, 127.0 x 315.7 cm. (each)
Purchase: Funds given by Mr. and Mrs. Arthur B. Baer   4:1970

THE SNOW RABBIT
Suzuki Harunobu, 1725-1770
Ukiyo-e wood block print, 28.1 x 21.3 cm.
Purchase 274:1955

A BEAUTY
Torii Kiyomitsu I, 1735-1785
Ukiyo e wood block print, 39.2 x 17.5 cm.
Purchase 283:1955

THE ACTOR
NAKAYAMA TOMISABURO
AS MIYAGINO
Toshusai Sharaku, active 1794-95
Ukiyo-e wood block print
36.8 x 24.8 cm.
Purchase 1045:1920

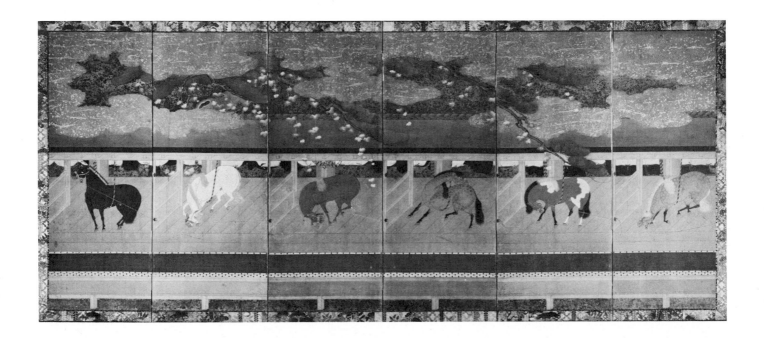

COVERED BOX
Attributed to Shibata Zeshin, 1807-1891
Lacquered wood with *maki-e* decoration
Width: 18.1 cm.
Purchase 592:1961

FLOWER HUNTING MURAL, 1958/65
Shiko Munakata, 1905-1975
Wood block print, 142.5 x 170.8 cm.
Gift of Shiko Munakata   12:1965

SUN GOD, SURYA
Indian, Mathura, Kushan Period, 2nd-3rd century
Red sandstone, Height: 26.6 cm.
Purchase and Friends Fund 3:1970

DEVATA, 3rd-5th century
North Indian, Gandhara
Stucco, traces of polychrome
Height: 24.1 cm.
Purchase 30:1931

HEAD OF BUDDHA, 3rd-5th century
North Indian, Gandhara
Stucco, traces of polychrome
Height: 45.7 cm.
Purchase 43:1931

HEAD OF A KING
3rd-5th century
North Indian, Gandhara
Stucco, Height: 19.7 cm.
Purchase 29:1931

BODHISATTVA, 3rd-4th century
North Indian, Gandhara
Schist, Height: 44.8 cm.
Gift of J. Lionberger Davis   22:1954

PARVATI
North Indian, Malwa, 12th century
Sandstone, Height: 54.0 cm.
Purchase 25:1971

SARDULA
Indian, 10th-11th century
Sandstone, Height: 77.5 cm.
Gift of Miss Martha I. Love 70:1965

Opposite
ARDHANARISVARA
South Indian, Chola Period, 10th-11th century
Granite, Height: 112.5 cm.
Purchase: Friends Fund   70:1962

PARVATI
South Indian, Chola Period, 11th century
Bronze, Height: 68.0 cm.
Purchase: Funds given by
The Merrill Trust Foundation   146:1966

VISHNU
South Indian, Chola Period, 10th century
Bronze, Height: 44.7 cm.
Purchase 2:1964

SHIVA NATARAJA, South Indian, Chola Period, 12th century, Bronze, Height: 87.0 cm., Purchase: W. K. Bixby Fund   4:1938

VAJRASATTVA, ADI-BUDDHA
Nepalese, 11th century
Gilt copper alloy, Height: 16.2 cm.
Purchase: W. K. Bixby Fund   25:1968

SKANDA-KARTTIKEYA
Nepalese, 12th-14th century
Gilt bronze, gemstones
Height: 15.9 cm.
Purchase: W. K. Bixby Fund
24:1971

AMITAYUS
Indian, Bengal, 12th-14th century
Copper alloy, gold and silver inlay
Height: 13.0 cm.
Gift of J. Lionberger Davis   107:1965

TANTRIC BUDDHIST DEITY
FORM OF AVALOKITESVARA
Kashmiri, 8th-9th century
Bronze, copper and silver inlay, Height: 21.2 cm.
Gift of J. Lionberger Davis   256:1955

PLATE, 7th-8th century
Iranian, Sassanian (?)
Partially gilded silver
Diameter: 28.6 cm.
Purchase: Friends Fund   114:1954

PAGE FROM A KORAN
Mesopotamian, Iraq, 8th-9th century
Ink, color and gold on parchment, 19.0 x 28.7 cm.
Purchase 32:1948

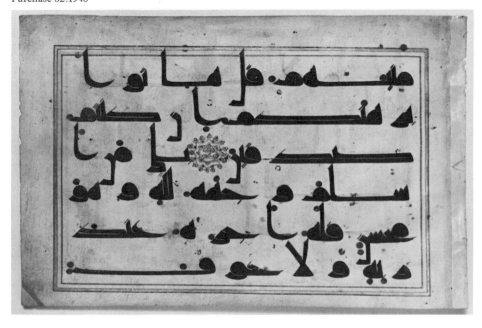

COVERED BOX
Iranian, Nishapur, 9th-10th century
Steatite, Height: 14.9 cm.
Purchase 71:1949

BOWL
Iranian, Nishapur, Samanid Period, 10th century
Underglaze slip painted earthenware, Diameter: 23.5 cm.
Purchase 29:1954

BOTTLE
Iranian, probably Nishapur, 10th century
Wheel-cut glass, Height: 13.5 cm.
Purchase: Friends Fund   23:1960

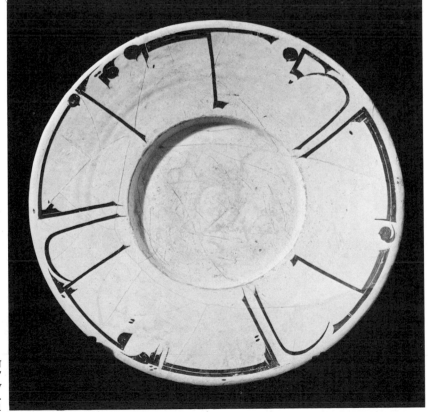

PLATE WITH KUFIC INSCRIPTION
"Deliberation before work protects you from regret"
Iranian, Samanid Period, 10th century
Underglaze slip painted earthenware, Diameter: 37.2 cm.
Purchase 283:1951

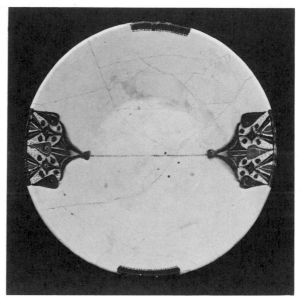

BOWL WITH KUFIC INSCRIPTION
Iranian, Samanid Period, 10th century
Underglaze slip painted earthenware
Diameter: 27.2 cm.
Purchase 148:1953

BOWL
Iranian, Samanid Period, 10th century
Underglaze slip painted earthenware
Diameter: 26.1 cm.
Purchase 149:1953

BOWL
Byzantine, 11th century
Glazed earthenware, incised decoration
Diameter: 25.0 cm.
Purchase 31:1971

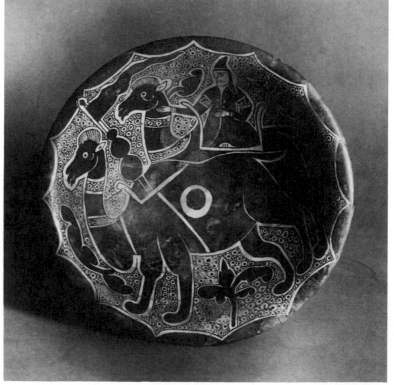

BOWL
Iraqi, Abbasid Period, 10th century
Overglaze luster painted earthenware
Diameter: 34.5 cm.,Purchase 16:1937

INCENSE BURNER
Iranian, Seljuk Period, 12th century
Bronze, Height: 17.8 cm.
Purchase: Eliza McMillan Fund 245:1952

BOTTLE
Syrian(?), 11th-12th century
Glass, Height: 28.6 cm.
Purchase 104:1921

PLATE, LAKABI WARE
Iranian, Seljuk Period, 12th century
Carved and glazed earthenware, Diameter: 28.1 cm.
Purchase 17:1937

KETTLE
Iranian, Seljuk Period, 12th century
Engraved bronze, Diameter: 20.7 cm.
Gift of J. Lionberger Davis 18:1954

LAMP HOLDER
Iranian, Seljuk Period, 12th century
Bronze, turquoise inlay, Height: 18.7 cm.
Gift of J. Lionberger Davis   17:1954

BOWL
Iranian, Seljuk Period, late 12th-early 13th century
Overglaze enameled and gilded earthenware
Diameter: 19.9 cm.
Purchase: W. K. Bixby Fund   41:1954

TANKARD
Iranian, Seljuk Period, early 13th century
Overglaze enameled earthenware
Height: 13.3 cm.
Purchase: W. K. Bixby Fund   163:1952

BOTTLE
Iranian, Seljuk Period, late 12th-early 13th century
Overglaze enameled, gilded earthenware, Height: 15.8 cm.
Gift of Mr. and Mrs. Samuel C. Davis   19:1937

SPOUTED JAR
Iranian, Seljuk Period, mid-13th century
Turquoise glazed and gilded earthenware
Height: 14.0 cm.
Gift of Mr. and Mrs. Joseph L. Werner 43:1936

BOWL
Iranian, Seljuk Period, early 13th century
Underglaze blue and black painted earthenware
Diameter: 20.0 cm.
Purchase 282:1951

BOWL WITH POETRY IN NASKHI SCRIPT
Iranian, Seljuk Period, early 13th century
Underglaze blue and overglaze
Gold luster painted earthenware
Diameter: 32.5 cm.
Gift of The Olsen Foundation 69:1953

عليه كبريتا وملحا ودعه في الآنون آما كتين ومنهم من ستعمل الكبريت

وحد الا انه لا يجوز في ذلك ومنهم من يلطخ المسامين بالشب والكبريت

والخل وتحرقها قدر من طين ومنهم من يصير المسامير في قدر

من نحاس ورش على المسامير خلا محرقها • وبعد احراقهما من يرش عليها الخل

من ما بنه ثم خرج ثم يفعل ايضا ويفعل بها ذلا بالله فاذا كان ذلك رفع

واجود ما يكون من النحاس المحرق ما كان من المدنه التي يقال لها مبس

TWO DOCTORS PREPARING A MEDICINE, 1224, Page from a *Materia Medica* by Dioscurides, Attributed to Abdallah ibn al-Fadl, Mesopotamian, Iraq, Baghdad school, Ink, color and gold on paper, 31.7 x 22.6 cm., Purchase 179:1955

Preceding page
CANDLESTICK
Iranian, 14th century
Bronze with silver inlay, Height: 29.2 cm.
Purchase 43:1926

BOWL, SULTANABAD WARE
Iranian, Ilkahanid Period, 1st half 14th century
Underglaze slip painted and carved earthenware
Diameter: 22.1 cm.
Purchase 50:1919

CASKET
Iranian, 14th century
Bronze with silver inlay, Height: 13.3 cm.
Purchase 42:1926

SWORD HILT
Iranian, 13th-14th(?) century
Gold, Width: 12.4 cm.
Purchase 45:1924

COVERED BOX
Iranian, 14th century
Bronze with silver inlay, Height: 27.9 cm.
Purchase 39:1926

BAHRAM GUR VISITING THE TATAR PRINCESS
AT THE GREEN PALACE
Iranian, School of Bihzad, mid-16th century
Ink, color and gold on paper, 25.8 x 15.3 cm.
Gift of J. Lionberger Davis   397:1952

HUNTING SCENE
Iranian, 16th century
Ink, washes on paper
16.1 x 23.8 cm.
Purchase 30:1948

FRONTISPIECE OF A MANUSCRIPT
Iranian, 16th century
Ink, color and gold on paper, 43.6 x 30.5 cm.
Gift of J. Lionberger Davis   387:1952

A CUPBEARER
School of Risa-i-Albaassi, Iranian, 17th century
Ink, color and gold on paper, 39.0 x 26.3 cm.
Purchase 2:1942

DAGGER, early 17th century
Iranian, Ispahan
Steel, Length: 34.3 cm.
Purchase 14:1922

DAGGER, 17th century
Iranian, Ispahan
Steel, ivory and gold, Length: 33.7 cm.
Purchase 13:1922

CANDLE HOLDER, early 17th century
Iranian, Ispahan
Brass, Height: 31.4 cm.
Purchase 86:1923

ASTROLABE
Made by Muhammad Amin ibn Muhammad Tahir
Engraved designs by Abd al-A'imma
Iranian, ca. 1715
Brass, Diameter: 18.1 cm.
Purchase 41:1926

HELMET
Iranian, 18th century
Steel with gold inlay, Height: 66.0 cm.
Purchase 70:1921

PLATE FROM A SET OF BODY ARMOR
Iranian, Ispahan, A.H. 1189 (A.D. 1775)
Gold inlaid steel, Height: 34.9 cm.
Purchase 34:1915

A SEIGE IN ONE OF THE WARS OF HULAGU KHAN
Khem Karan, period of Akbar, 2nd half 16th century
Ink, color and gold on paper, 34.8 x 22.2 cm.
Gift of J. Lionberger Davis   388:1952

THE EMPEROR BABUR HOLDING COURT
Reign of Akbar, 1556-1606
Ink, color and gold on paper, 33.0 x 21.0 cm.
Gift of J. Lionberger Davis   25:1958

TWO LOVERS, late 16th century
Ink, color and gold on silk
39.7 x 28.2 cm.
Purchase 42:1952

THE EMPEROR JAHANGIR HOLDING COURT
Period of Jahangir, ca. 1607-10
Ink, color and gold on paper, 22.4 x 12.9 cm.
Gift of J. Lionberger Davis   399:1952

JOSEPH TELLING HIS DREAMS
TO HIS FATHER
Period of Jahangir, ca. 1610
Ink, color and gold on paper, 42.2 x 26.5 cm.
Gift of J. Lionberger Davis   403:1952

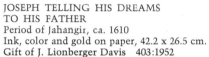

KHOSROW, SON OF NAZR MUHAMMED KHAN
Period of Jahangir, early 17th century
Ink, color and gold on paper, 38.0 x 25.0 cm.
Gift of J. Lionberger Davis   400:1952

THE EMPEROR AKBAR HUNTING
Period of Akbar or Jahangir, ca. 1600-1610
Ink, color and gold on paper, 19.0 x 13.2 cm.
Gift of J. Lionberger Davis   105:1953

THE EMPEROR SHAH JAHAN, Period of Shah Jahan, mid-17th century
Ink, color and gold on paper, 21.0 x 12.4 cm., Gift of J. Lionberger Davis 389:1952

LAILA AND MAJNUN
Period of Shah Jahan, mid-17th century
Ink, color and gold on paper, 30.0 x 19.7 cm.
Gift of J, Lionberger Davis   401:1952

RUG FRAGMENT
Period of Shah Jahan, mid-17th century
Silk, sehna knot, 58.4 x 27.9 cm.
Gift of James F. Ballard   73:1929

DAGGER, 17th century
Steel, gold and ivory
Length: 35.2 cm.
Purchase 51:1925

GEOMETRIC RUG, "CAIRENE" TYPE
Egyptian, Ottoman Period, 16th century
Wool, sehna knot, 193.0 x 137.2 cm.
Gift of James F. Ballard   121:1929

COMPARTMENT RUG FRAGMENT
Syro-Egyptian, probably Damascus
Ottoman Period, 17th century
Wool, sehna knot, 167.6 x 91.4 cm.
Gift of James F. Ballard   110:1929

BASIN
Egyptian (?), Ottoman Period, 16th-17th century
Bronze with silver inlay, Diameter: 55.6 cm.
Purchase 50:1927

PART OF A PANEL OF TILES, IZNIK WARE
Ottoman Period, last quarter 16th century
Overglaze polychrome enameled earthenware
128.0 x 57.4 cm.
Purchase: W. K. Bixby Fund   47:1956

ARABESQUE RUG, "LOTTO" TYPE
Western Anatolia, Ottoman Period
Late 16th-early 17th century
Wool, ghiordes knot, 170.2 x 109.2 cm.
Gift of James F. Ballard   104:1929

PLATE, IZNIK WARE
Ottoman Period, mid-16th century
Overglaze polychrome enameled earthenware
Diameter: 36.0 cm.
Purchase 182:1951

Opposite
MEDALLION RUG, USHAK TYPE
Western Anatolia, Ottoman Period, late 16th-early 17th century
Wool, ghiordes knot, 315.0 x 228.6 cm.
Gift of James F. Ballard   98:1929

PRAYER RUG, "TRANSYLVANIAN" TYPE
Turkish (?), Ottoman Period, late 17th century
Wool, ghiordes knot, 160.0 x 124.5 cm.
Gift of James F. Ballard   92:1929

MEDALLION RUG, "HOLBEIN" TYPE
Western Anatolia, Ottoman Period, 16th or early 17th century
Wool, ghiordes knot, 198.1 x 121.9 cm.
Gift of James F. Ballard   106:1929

COMPARTMENT RUG, YURUK TYPE
Central Anatolia, Ottoman Period, 19th century
Wool, ghiordes knot, 185.4 x 121.9 cm.
Gift of James F. Ballard   89:1929

PRAYER RUG, LADIK TYPE
South-central Anatolia
Ottoman Period, 1st half 19th century
Wool, ghiordes knot, 198.1 x 115.6 cm.
Gift of Nellie Ballard White   311:1972

PRAYER RUG, MUDJUR TYPE
Central Anatolia
Ottoman Period, 2nd half 19th century
Wool, ghiordes knot, 185.4 x 134.6 cm.
Gift of James F. Ballard   108:1929

MASK, 300-600, Mexican, Central Highlands, Teotihuacan III Culture, Black stone, Height: 20.1 cm., Purchase 5:1948

SOLID FIGURINE, 800-500 B.C.
Mexican, Central Highlands, Tlatilco, type D-1
Earthenware, Height: 9.1 cm.
Purchase 294:1951

VESSEL IN THE FORM OF
A SLEEPING DOG
Thin-Orange Ware, 300-600
Mexican, Central Highlands
Teotihuacan III Culture
Earthenware, Height: 9.0 cm.
Anonymous Gift   108:1966

WARRIOR, 200 B.C. - A.D. 300
West Mexican, Colima
Painted earthenware, Height: 33.2 cm.
Purchase 131:1956

HOLLOW FIGURE, 800-200 B.C.
Mexican, Central Highlands, Morelos
Burnished earthenware, Height: 42.7 cm.
Gift of Allan Gerdau   186:1953

THIN-STONE HEAD
HUMAN FACE IN JAWS OF SERPENT, 700-900
Guatemalan, Pacific Coast, Cotzumalhuapa Culture
Green stone, Height: 30.5 cm.
Gift of Morton D. May   98:1968

XIPE TOTEC, 700-1000
Mexican, Gulf Coast, Remojadas Culture
Earthenware, Height: 50.5 cm.
Gift of Mr. and Mrs. Milton Tucker   333:1962

SEATED FIGURE, 1000-1200, Mexican, Yucatan, Toltec-Maya Culture
Stone, plaster, paint, Height: 63.5 cm., Gift of Morton D. May 95:1968

TLALOC MASK, 1250-1450
Mexican, Mixtec Culture
Turquoise and shell on stone
Height: 13.6 cm.
Gift of Morton D. May   96:1968

FOOTED INCENSE BOWL, 1250-1450
Cholula Polychrome Ware
Mexican, Mixtec Culture
Painted earthenware, Height: 11.1 cm.
Purchase 86:1950

Preceding page
PLATE, 1250-1450
Cholula Polychrome Ware
Mexican, Mixtec Culture
Painted earthenware
Diameter: 22.9 cm.
Purchase 85:1950

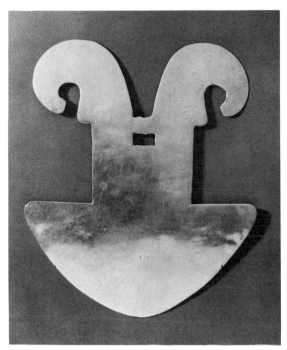

BIRD PENDANT, 1000-1500
Panamanian, Veraguas Culture
Gold, Width: 13.2 cm.
Purchase 163:1944

CEREMONIAL KNIFE, 1st-5th century
Colombian, Calima or Tolima Culture
Gold with some copper, Height: 17.6 cm.
Purchase 247:1966

PENDANT, 500-1000
Colombian, Quimbaya Culture
Gold, Height: 9.6 cm.
Purchase 153:1944

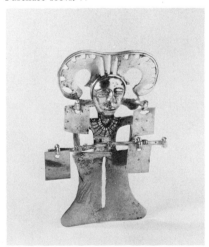

FOOTED DISH WITH
CROCODILE-GOD DESIGN, 1000-1500
Panamanian, Veraguas Culture
Painted earthenware, Diameter: 25.0 cm.
Purchase 129:1952

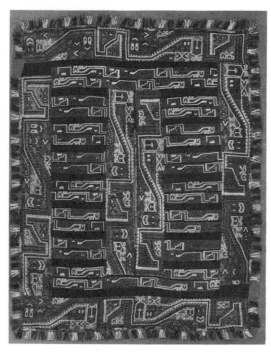

PONCHO, 500-200 B.C.
South Coast, Paracas Culture
Wool embroidery on cotton, 76.5 x 60.0 cm.
Purchase: Friends Fund and Maymar Corporation   24:1956

SHIRT, 1000-1450
South Coast, Ica Culture
Wool, tapestry weave, Width: 125.0 cm.
Purchase 284:1949

MANTLE, 500-200 B.C., South Coast, Paracas Culture
Wool embroidery on cotton, Width: 260.0 cm., Purchase: Friends Fund and Maymar Corporation   21:1956

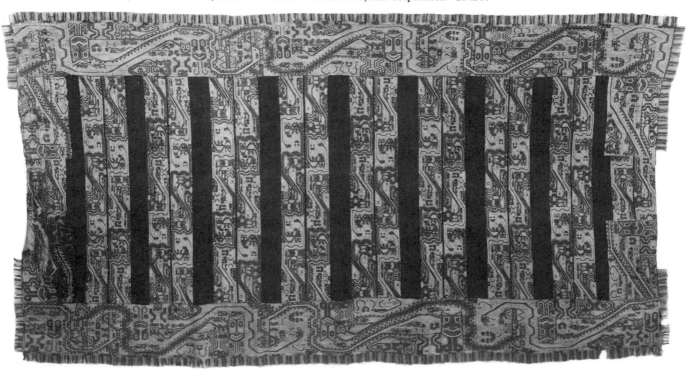

STIRRUP-SPOUT BOTTLE
DEPICTING A SEATED NOBLEMAN, 200-500
North Coast, Mochica IV Culture
Painted earthenware, Height: 23.4 cm.
Gift of J. Lionberger Davis   124:1954

PORTRAIT BOTTLE, 300-100 B.C.
Far North Coast, Vicus Culture
Painted earthenware, Height: 20.5 cm.
Gift of Morton D. May by exchange   109:1966

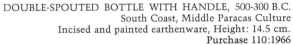

DOUBLE-SPOUTED BOTTLE WITH HANDLE, 500-300 B.C.
South Coast, Middle Paracas Culture
Incised and painted earthenware, Height: 14.5 cm.
Purchase 110:1966

DOUBLE-SPOUTED "BOTTLE-BOWL," 1st-2nd century
South Coast, Early Nazca Culture
Polychrome painted earthenware, Height: 19.3 cm.
Gift of J. Lionberger Davis   133:1954

HOLLOW FEMALE FIGURE
Inca Period, 1438-1532, Silver, Height: 6.2 cm.
Gift of J. Lionberger Davis   168:1954

HOLLOW LLAMA EFFIGY
Inca Period, 1438-1532, Gold, Height: 6.1 cm.
Gift of J. Lionberger Davis   166:1954

GOBLET, 2nd half 16th century
Post-Conquest Inca
Polychrome inlaid wood, Height: 16.6 cm.
Gift of J. Lionberger Davis   123:1954

PALETTE WITH DOUBLE RATTLESNAKE MOTIF, ca. 1400, Alabama, late Mississippian, Southern Cult
Engraved limestone, Diameter: 27.0 cm., Gift of Mr. and Mrs. A. J. Koller   228:1973

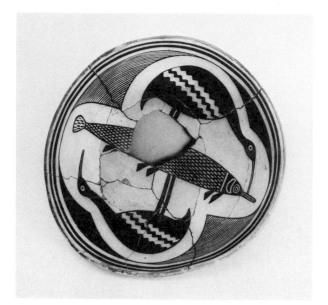

BOWL WITH DESIGN OF CRANES AND GARFISH, 1000-1300
New Mexico, Mimbres Culture
Painted earthenware, Diameter: 24.4 cm.
Purchase 111:1944

BOWL WITH BAT DESIGN, 1000-1300
New Mexico, Mimbres Culture
Painted earthenware, Diameter: 23.1 cm.
Purchase 113:1944

BLANKET, 19th century
Southern Alaska, Chilkat Tribe
Wool, wood fiber and
Puffin beaks, Width: 90.0 cm.
Gift of Mr. Charles M. Rice
51:1924

HEAD OF AN OBA, before 1550, Nigeria, Benin City, Bronze, Height: 20.6 cm., Purchase 12:1936

HEAD OF AN OBA, 1550-1650, Nigeria, Benin City, Bronze, Height: 29.5 cm., Purchase 674:1949

HEDDLE PULLEY
Ivory Coast, Baule Tribe
Wood, Height: 19.8 cm.
Gift of Mr. and Mrs.
Alvin S. Novack   100:1958

MASK, Ivory Coast, Senufo Tribe
Wood, Height: 28.6 cm.
Purchase: Funds given by Howard F. Baer
140:1972

MASK
Ivory Coast, Baule Tribe
Painted wood, Height: 31.1 cm.
Gift of Mrs. Vladimir Golschmann   251:1972

PORO SOCIETY MASK
Liberia, Dan Tribe
Wood, Height: 20.5 cm.
Gift of Mr. and Mrs. Alvin S. Novack
90:1958

MASK
Gabon, Ogowe River
Painted wood, Height: 30.9 cm.
Gift of Mr. and Mrs. Alvin S. Novack   542:1956

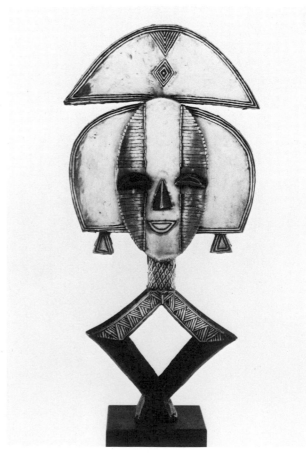

RELIQUARY FIGURE
Gabon, BaKota Tribe
Wood, brass and copper, Height: 58.3 cm.
Gift of Mr. and Mrs. Alvin S. Novack   69:1956

MASK
Cameroon, Cross River, Widekum Tribe
Wood, hide and hair, Height: 42.1 cm.
Purchase 26:1942

RELIQUARY FIGURE
Gabon, Fang Tribe
Wood and metal, Height: 49.4 cm.
Purchase 23:1942

STAFF FINIAL, SEATED FIGURE
Zaire or Angola, BaChokwe Tribe
Wood and metal, Height: 14.7 cm.
Purchase 24:1942

Opposite
CHIEF'S CHAIR
Zaire or Angola, BaChokwe Tribe
Wood and hide, Height: 74.0 cm.
Purchase 7:1943

FETISH FIGURE
Zaire, BaSonge Tribe
Wood, metal, shells, fiber, Height: 60.0 cm.
Gift of Morton D. May   156:1965

SHRINE FIGURE
Zaire, BaBembe Tribe
Wood and ivory, Height: 21.4 cm.
Purchase 25:1942

HEAD REST
Zaire, BaYaka Tribe
Wood, Length: 21.8 cm.
Purchase 20:1942

HELMET MASK
Zaire, BaSuku Tribe
Painted wood, Height: 32.2 cm.
Gift of Morton D. May   409:1955

ANCESTOR FIGURE
Zaire, BaLuba Tribe
Wood, Height: 68.0 cm.
Purchase 21:1942

STAFF-CLUB (detail), 19th century
Polynesian, Marquesas Islands
Wood, Length: 132.1 cm.
Purchase 128:1952

FEATHER CLOAK, 19th century
Polynesian, New Zealand, Maori Culture
Feathers and woven flax, Width: 70.0 cm.
Gift of Mrs. Paul Blackwelder   530:1957
Detail opposite

MALANGGAN MEMORIAL PLAQUE
HORNBILL WITH FLYING FISH, 19th century
Melanesian, New Ireland
Painted wood, Length: 152.0 cm.
Purchase 244:1952

MALANGGAN HELMET MASK, 19th century
Melanesian, New Ireland
Wood, plant fibers, Height: 45.2 cm.
Purchase 122:1952

Inquiries regarding works of art in the Museum's collections should be directed to the curatorial department. The curatorial staff and their specific areas of responsibility are listed in the bimonthly *Bulletin*.

The Richardson Memorial Library is a comprehensive art reference service with a collection in excess of 20,000 volumes including bound periodicals, auction catalogues and pamphlets, as well as archival material. The Library is available for use by the adult public.

Photographs and transparencies of works of art in the collections may be obtained through the photography manager for study purposes or for publication. The Museum reserves all rights of reproduction unless specifically granted in writing. Color slides of works of art in the collections, many accompanied by information packets, are available through the Teachers Resource Center. Reproduction from slides is not permitted.

Regular Museum publications include: the bimonthly *Bulletin*, containing articles on recent acquisitions and current exhibitions; *Museum Monographs*, a biannual collection of scholarly articles which elaborate on works of art in the Museum's collections; the *Annual Report*, with a full listing of works of art acquired during the year, as well as a financial statement and summary of the year's activities.

The Museum is open to the public:
Tuesday   2:30 - 9:30
Wednesday through Sunday   10:00 - 5:00
Closed Monday, Christmas Day, New Year's Day
Admission free

Business hours:
Monday through Friday   8:30 - 5:00

Address:
The St. Louis Art Museum
Forest Park
St. Louis, Missouri 63110

Telephone:
(314) 721-0067

PURCHASE FUNDS

W. K. Bixby Oriental Art Trust Fund
The Sidney and Sadie Cohen
    Foundation, Inc., Print Purchase Fund
Contemporary Art Society Fund
Decorative Arts Society Fund
The Friends of
    The St. Louis Art Museum Fund
Eliza McMillan Trust Fund

BENEFACTORS

Irene Catlin Allen
Helen and Arthur B. Baer
James F. Ballard
The Louis D. Beaumont Foundation
William K. Bixby
Mrs. Daniel Catlin
Sadie and Sidney S. Cohen
J. Lionberger Davis
Samuel C. Davis
Edward A. and Anna Busch Faust
Leicester Busch and Mary Plant Faust
Cora Liggett Fowler
Mr. and Mrs. H. C. Grigg
Barbara K. and Joseph A. Helman
Marie and G. Gordon Hertslet
Arthur C. Hoskins
Louise Woodruff Johnston
Mary Ranken Jordan and
    Ettie A. Jordan
    Charitable Foundation
John Allan Love and Mary Potter Love
Martha Irene Love
Edward Mallinckrodt, Sr.
Morton D. May
Wilbur D. May
Eliza McMillan
Alvin S. Novack
John M. Olin
Joseph Pulitzer
Joseph Pulitzer, Jr.
Henry V. Putzel
Marcus and Bettie W. Rice
Mary D. Richardson
The St. Louis Post-Dispatch Foundation
Sydney M. Shoenberg, Sr.
Sydney M. Shoenberg, Jr.
Shoenberg Foundation, Inc.
John E. Simon
Etta E. Steinberg
Horace M. Swope
Florence S. and Richard K. Weil
Nellie Ballard White

Anonymous Donors
Mrs. Frederic W. Allen
Mrs. John S. Ames
Mr. Winslow Ames
Mrs. H. B. Armstrong
Mr. and Mrs. Edwin M. Ashcraft III
Bachstitz Gallery
Mrs. Arthur B. Baer
Mr. and Mrs. Arthur B. Baer
Mr. Howard F. Baer
Mr. and Mrs. Howard F. Baer
Miss Berenice C. Ballard
The heirs of
    Miss Berenice Ballard
Mr. James F. Ballard
Mrs. Philip Barney
Miss Leona J. Beckmann
Mrs. Paul Blackwelder
Mr. Albert Blair (Bequest)
Mrs. John Brodhead, Jr.
Mr. Daniel K. Catlin
Mrs. Daniel K. Catlin
Mr. and Mrs. Norman B. Champ, Jr.
Mrs. F. H. (Beatrice Lindell) Cook
Mrs. Robert Corley
Mr. William Corman (Bequest)
Mr. J. Lionberger Davis
Mr. Samuel C. Davis (Bequest)
Mrs. Samuel C. Davis
Mr. and Mrs. Samuel C. Davis
Mr. and Mrs. Theodore P. Desloge
Draper and Draper
Mrs. Arthur C. Drefs
Sir Joseph Duveen
Mrs. Wright Prescott Edgerton
Miss Imogene Evans (Bequest)
Mr. Leicester Busch Faust
Mrs. J. Russell Forgan
Mrs. Cora Liggett Fowler (Bequest)
Mr. and Mrs. L. Calvin Fulenwider
The Garden Club of St. Louis
Mrs. Clifford W. Gaylord
Mr. Allan Gerdau
Mrs. Charles C. Gifford
Miss Nancy W. Gilmartin
Mr. and Mrs. Ira Glackens
Mrs. Max A. Goldstein
Mrs. Vladimir Golschmann
Miss Elizabeth Green
Mr. and Mrs. Ronald K. Greenberg

Prof. and Mrs. Theo Haimann
Mr. and Mrs. Stanley Hanks
Mr. Henry C. Harvey
Mr. F. Lee Hawes
Mr. Richard S. Hawes III
Mr. and Mrs. Joseph A. Helman
Mr. and Mrs. G. Gordon Hertslet
Mrs. Marie Setz Hertslet (Bequest)
Mrs. H. Lionel Herzfelder
Mrs. Arthur Hoskins
Beatrice T. Hoskins Trust
Mr. James H. Hyde
Mr. and Mrs. Roland Jester
Mr. Andrew W. Johnson
Mrs. Jackson Johnson
Mary Ranken Jordan and Ettie A. Jordan
    Charitable Foundation
Mrs. I. D. Kelley
Mr. and Mrs. Richard Kent
M. Knoedler & Co., Inc.
Mrs. Hugo A. Koehler
Miss Stella Koetter
Mr. and Mrs. A. J. Koller
Miss Effie C. Kuhn
Miss Stella Kuhn
Lafayette Federal
Mr. Oliver M. Langenberg
Lanlee Realty Co.
Lea-Thi-Ta Study Group
Mr. Virgil A. Lewis
Ezra H. Linley Fund
Mr. and Mrs. Hugh A. Logan
Mrs. Christine Graham Long (Bequest)
Mr. C. T. Loo
Mr. John Allan Love
Miss Martha I. Love
Mr. Sanford N. and
    Mrs. Priscilla R. McDonnell
Mrs. William A. McDonnell
Mrs. Norman Frederick Mack
Mr. Edward Mallinckrodt, Sr. (Bequest)
Mr. and Mrs. Robert F. Mathews
Mr. Morton D. May
Mr. and Mrs. Morton D. May
Mr. Morton J. May
Maymar Corporation
The Measuregraph Company
Mr. Charles E. and Mrs. Mary Merrill
The Charles E. Merrill Trust Foundation
Mrs. R. L. Metcalfe

Mr. John P. Meyer
Mr. Stratford Lee Morton
Mrs. Stratford Lee Morton
Mr. Shiko Munakata
Mr. and Mrs. James Myles
National Endowment for the Arts
Mr. and Mrs. Alvin S. Novack
John M. Olin Charitable Trust
The Olsen Foundation
Miss Martha O'Neil
Orbit Corporation
Mr. and Mrs. William R. Orthwein
Mr. William Pagenstecher
Mrs. William S. Paley
Mr. and Mrs. Christian B. Peper
Mrs. Eugene A. Perry
Mr. Oliver F. Peters (Bequest)
Mr. J. Harold Pettus
Mr. Henry B. Pflager
Miss Nellie V. Plant (Bequest)
The Mary Powell Tribute Fund
Mr. Vincent Price
Mr. Joseph Pulitzer
Mr. Joseph Pulitzer, Jr.
Mr. and Mrs. Joseph Pulitzer, Jr.
Mr. Alphonse Raes
Miss Lillie B. Randell
Lillie B. Randell Fund
Mr. Charles M. Rice
Mr. and Mrs. Marcus Rice
Mr. and Mrs. George S. Rosborough, Jr.
Mr. Theodore Schempp
Mr. and Mrs. George H. Schlapp
Miss Cornelia Scott
Mrs. Mason Scudder
Mrs. Warren McKinney Shapleigh
Mr. and Mrs. Warren McKinney
  Shapleigh
Mrs. John F. Shepley
Family of Mrs. Judith B. Shepley
Mrs. Bradford Shinkle

Shoenberg Foundation, Inc.
Mr. Sydney M. Shoenberg, Sr.
Mr. Sydney M. Shoenberg, Jr.
Mr. and Mrs. John E. Simon
Miss G. C. Spalding
Mrs. James H. Spencer
Mrs. Frank Spiekerman
Steinberg Charitable Fund
Mrs. Mark C. Steinberg
Mr. Charles Henry Stix
Mr. Charles Henry Stix (Bequest)
General and Mrs. Leif J. Sverdrup
Mrs. John L. Swasey
Mr. Horace M. Swope
Mr. Horace M. Swope (Bequest)
Sycamore Tree Trust
Mr. Edgar Lackland Taylor
Mr. Joseph Ternbach
Mr. and Mrs. Lansing W. Thoms
Thoms Pontiac, Inc.
Mr. and Mrs. Philip H. Tomlinson
Mr. and Mrs. Joseph L. Tucker
Mr. and Mrs. Milton H. Tucker
Mr. Curt Valentin (Bequest)
Mrs. Elizabeth Von Weise
Ellis Wainwright Fund
Mrs. Audrey Faust Wallace
Colonel James H. Wear
The Weil Charitable Foundation
Mrs. Richard K. Weil
Mr. and Mrs. Richard K. Weil
Emelie Weindal Bequest Fund
Mr. Joseph L. Werner
Mr. and Mrs. Joseph L. Werner
Western Electric Company
Mrs. Nellie Ballard White
Mr. and Mrs. Anthony Wilson
Winfield Foundation
Mrs. Neal S. Wood
The Young Presidents Organization

Bingham
Captured by the Indians
1848   147:1962
not good

Landscape with Cattle, 1846   410:1923
orig. overall
not exciting, dull in
subj. + color

Self-Portrait   57.1934
1834/35
plastic-like

The Wood Boat 1850   14:1951
orig. overall
secure
colors soft

Jolly Flatboatmen in Port, 1857
orig. overall - secure   123:1944
muted coloration

County Election   185/5 2   124:1944
good condition
colors not brilliant

Raftsmen Playing Cards 1847   50:1939
soft colors
clear delineation
good cond.